# The Girl Who Runs Backwards

# The Girl Who Runs Backwards

## Reflections in a rear view mirror

Anne Ashworth

The Pentland Press Limited
Edinburgh • Cambridge • Durham • USA

First published in 1997 by
The Pentland Press Ltd.
1 Hutton Close
South Church
Bishop Auckland
Durham

British Library Cataloguing in Publication Data.
A Catalogue record for this book is available
from the British Library.

ISBN 1 85821 4904

Typeset by CBS, Felixstowe, Suffolk
Printed and bound by Antony Rowe Ltd., Chippenham

For Perri and Catriona

# CONTENTS

# LIST OF POEMS

# *ACKNOWLEDGEMENTS*

Some of the poems in this book have appeared elsewhere, though in all cases copyright remains with the author. However, acknowledgement is made to the editors of

> *Orbis*
> *Other Poetry*
> *The Rialto*
> *Staple*
> *The Wide Skirt*

and to the publishers of

> *Mirrorwork.* Anne Ashworth. Envoi Poets
> *Surfing: women on the Sea of Faith.* Sea of Faith publns.

The quotation from Mary Warnock in the Preface is used with the kind permission of Blackwell Publishers.

# *PREFACE*

This memoir is set in a very odd form. Eccentric, even perverse, some might say. Why insert poetry in a prose narrative? Tiresome, irritating, if the reader is not a poetry lover. Alternatively, why not just a book of poems? Poetry shouldn't need prose to prop it up.

I sympathise with both views. But in this very personal document, in which I attempt the risky project of being honest with myself about myself, both forms are necessary to me. The narrative provides the structural frame - and, I hope, occasional light relief - while the poetry probes deeper layers. My ideal reader, who probably does not exist, will read steadily through the lot, and perhaps at length appreciate my reasons for the form.

The poems were not written specially for the memoir; I have drawn on already existing poems. The prose is therefore newer than the verse, but paradoxically the poems (with a single exception) were written much later than the period covered by the narrative.

Mary Warnock writes:
'For an autobiography, or autobiographical novel, to work, it is not necessary that its author should have led an "important" or an "interesting" life, judged by the standards imported from politics or social history, or any of the sciences. What it needs is the search for truth, through memory and the interpreting imagination . . . Because human beings are bound together by sympathy, the reflection in the glass is necessarily not of one person only. The common, the shared and the general is to be found in the particular, if the particular is truthfully described, and with imagination. To discover such a common truth is an intrinsic good.'
(IMAGINATION AND TIME, Blackwell 1994)

To that discovery, this book, however falteringly, aspires.

*Anne Ashworth*, 1996

# THE GIRL WHO RUNS BACKWARDS

An awkward gait and one that places her
at perpetual disadvantage.

Perhaps it began when they told her about the natives
at the bottom of the garden.
You must be respectful to fairies
she understood
and wary too.
They might not like being looked at.
So she backed off skilfully down the lawn until
she found it was true
about the strange inhabitants
and about the magic
as she poked an experimental finger tip
into a dewbead.
She didn't tell her mother
who anyway was a long way off.

If you run backwards hard enough
she reasoned
you might reach rainbow ends as well.

So she went on practising.

You can see her now any day
stretching her arms
to puzzled friends and lovers.
*I'm coming she cries*
or *Touch me*
from the end of the avenue.

## The Girl Who Runs Backwards

If you think it worth it
to watch her long enough
as she twinkles away over the rounding earth
the last vestige vanishing on the horizon
might be her finger tips.

# 1. Keyholes

In the beginning was the poetry. Words have been my life; but before my own feeble language could grapple with the world, before adult conversation became intelligible, there was the sound of poetry.

My mother was an elocutionist. It seems an archaic designation, faintly ridiculous. I doubt if such a class of person exists today. She spoke – no, *performed* would be her own word – prose as well as verse, but it was all poetry. At home, as she went about the domestic chores that always irked her, she rehearsed. Great rolling rhythms washed over me, vowels that vibrated over her vocal cords, consonants that cut crisp blades of air, emotions travelling on ordered flightpaths along the airwaves. Speech: it was the first of arts, long before that johnny-come-lately means of communication, poor limping writing.

Andromache, Ophelia, Hiawatha – the names curled over my ears like coloured ribbons. 'You murdering ministers', 'O soft embalmer', 'Minnehaha' – it was all laughing-water, meaningless but marvellous, flowing and falling, pounding, enchanting. What need of music to gild the lily? We had no music, not even a wireless set. My mother cared little for it. She was indeed overtly contemptuous of what she considered the spoiling of poetry by setting it to music, the ruin of drama turned grotesquely into opera.

Emma Cleator had little formal schooling. Her small provincial private school had provided her with hardly more than an opportunity for unstructured unsupervised reading. She emerged with an odd reverence for higher education and a private rose coloured dream of Oxford which, whether deliberately or not, she contrived to transfer to my childish imagination. Cruelly, as it was to turn out.

What she cherished was words, above all the sound of words. From a family with few intellectual expectations, least of all for the only girl, she had somehow found her way to London to study under Katie Thomas, speech tutor to the stammerer King George VI. Those London days were champagne to dumpy Emma from Fleetwood, hitherto 'fat Emma'. She stored up the sophistication, the city lights, the images of West End theatre and Lyons Corner Houses, as a camel stores water or a squirrel nuts. Well that she did, for there was desert or winter ahead, and she had need of her memories. But she had health, irrational optimism, a firm belief in her professionalism and an astonished delight in her only, late-born child.

Though a voracious reader, mother was not, I must own, a critical one. I still blush to recall some of her reciter's stock in trade. Among the earliest 'pieces' I was set to learn and perform were the verses of Rose Fyleman, now remembered – if at all – as the perpetrator of
There are fairies at the bottom of our garden.
Rose Fyleman may be said to have created the conventional fairy as Dickens created the conventional Christmas. Fairies in Celtic and Teutonic legend were robust, often malevolent creatures. Fyleman's emasculated gauzy-winged diminutives had at least the merit of inspiring no terror – so that when the slightly older child next door suggested that these denizens might indeed be in residence, though I struggled between disbelief and doubt it was rather in hope than in fear that I considered the possibility. The argument shapes itself lucidly in my memory. My mother had firmly explained that fairies were fictional. But would a grown-up really know about such matters? My six-year-old neighbour was almost certainly patronising me, deliberately teasing and misleading. Or could she just possibly know something important? I approached the bottom of the garden with careful respect. After all, the flowers were quite evidently magic. Such colours, such shapes, the lupins and dahlias; such scents, the catmint and pinks; how they appeared and vanished! Given such magic, surely the world must be full of evanescent wonders. That conviction is with me still.

4

*Keyholes*

It is easy to remember infancy, because so much is forgotten. This first chapter composes itself. The selection is fully automated. It is like looking at a starry sky. There they are, those pin points, those small illuminations, unconnected, minute, identifiable.

There was, literally, one such tiny lightshape. Its source was a ventilator high on my bedroom wall, and its small glow in the darkness excited and disquieted me. Perhaps I enquired and was given the word 'ventilator'. But children easily confuse strange words. Somehow another V became conflated with the ventilator; the mental trickster shuffled the cards, and that faint light on the wall became a volcano. I had no idea what a volcano was, hardly even associated it with fire, but I was certain that it was a matter for terror, How many nights did I lie trembling? Yet it was air, it was light, it might have been comfort. Are there other horrors which, properly understood, might turn out to be ventilators? I have known one or two.

Pinpoints of light, keyholes to the past. One actual keyhole I recall too vividly, even now. The picture is clear, the feeling that accompanies it as distasteful as ever. My mother is in the dining room, teaching an adult pupil, so my father and I are banished. From another room I emerge into the hall – and chance upon my father bending eye to keyhole at the dining room door. To be sure, there may have been no keyhole; he may just have been listening. He said nothing, unless it were 'Shsh'. Neither did I. Racked with an awareness I could not articulate, I fled on small four-year-old legs to my bedroom.

Disillusionment. My first awakening to the imperfections of humankind, to the knowledge that parents had clay feet. Who was this eavesdropper? My daddy? An unexplained revulsion, like nausea, rose in me: a new feeling, to which I could as yet give no name. I recognised it later: contempt.

That contempt never left me. In later years, observing this weak and foolish man, I collected evidence to reinforce my harsh judgment. He was not evil, and I did not hate him; but nor, after the earliest years, did I love him, devoted though he always was to me. My relief at his death when I was twenty-five was incalculable. That too remains with me. Yet now, in my sixties less willing to pass judgment on anyone, I dare to think again of James Henry Roe. Who was he? What was his own family background? Unlike my mother, he never reminisced, except to mention that he came from Stoke and knew the pottery industry. Nor could my mother ever be drawn.

'Your father doesn't like to talk about his home,' was all she would ever say. And once, explaining why alcohol was never allowed in our household, 'His father and mother drank. That's why he won't.' For the first twenty-five years of my life, both my parents appeared models of conventional rectitude.

Through later childhood I puzzled occasionally – not often – about my father. Why was he so much older than other children's fathers? Why had he not fought in the Great War? Why did he keep losing jobs? Was there a mystery of some kind?

But at four, of course, I was still also daddy's girl, allowed to draw silly faces and call them 'Funny Daddy', taken for walks, lifted to post letters. The walks had their problems. 'Walk properly!' was the staid fifty-year-old accountant's repeated exhortation, insensitive to a four-year-old's absolute need to jump, skip, run.

One cannot blame James Henry for that, still less for his bewilderment as I tried to describe my antics. Quite precisely, in my own terms, I explained that a run of a certain length and speed was 'a green run', that a specified kind of leap was 'an orange jump'. Similarly, days of the week had their individual, known colours. Apparently this synaesthetic sense is not uncommon among young children. Psychologists are still baffled by studies of adults in whom the phenomenon persists. I am not one of those, but childhood memories are clear enough to persuade me that children may perhaps experience some perceptions not normally available to their elders. What price the fairies in the garden? We are shut out, like Alice, having only keyhole vision of the garden; barred, like Adam and Eve, from some antique pre-rational knowledge. So can we keep, as Edwin Muir hoped, 'one foot in Eden still'? It has been my lifelong endeavour to preserve mine. I am the girl who runs backwards.

Pictures help. Stories help. Poetry, for me, is indispensable. I cannot say what books my mother first read to me, but those readings are my earliest and most cherished memories. That rich dark chocolate voice, the voice which (as I later knew) with only its own skilled amplification could subdue and enthral large audiences, wrought its magic for me alone. The A.A. Milne verses were early favourites, and the Alice books. Better still were Kipling's *Just So Stories*, with their hypnotic prose, idea-tickling verses and zany puzzle pictures. I could probably still recite *The Sing-Song of Old Man Kangaroo* from memory. Soon we were on to the *Jungle Books*, so that the Mowgli tales, half comprehended, sang in my head before I could read 'The cat sat on the mat'. Kipling's prose laid the basis for later appreciation of prose rhythms. He was a great stylist.

Never patronise children, my mother insisted. They love the sound of words, mysterious long words they cannot understand but roll voluptuously over their tongues and through their memories. She was right. I recall a snatch from some long-forgotten book of rhymes, declaimed ad nauseam by me at age seven:
> The dinky bird's bravuras and staccatos are so sweet,
> His roulades, appoggiaturas and robustos so complete
> That the youth of every nation, be they near or far away,
> Find especial delectation in that gladsome roundelay.

Parents who do not read aloud not only sell their children short, they deprive themselves. When my turn came to read to my son, it was a joy reborn, and the richer for adult understanding. Nowadays he and I, thirty-something and sixty-something, in our rare times together spend happy

7

hours reading aloud to one another. He is a better reader than I, though I hope I am not without skill. His grandmother would have rejoiced.

And so the priorities, the motivating principles, were set in place: words, poetry, stories, pictures, colours, notions. That's a vague old-fashioned word: notions. I choose it both for its period flavour and for its hazy outline. Notions are less sharp, less articulated, than ideas. They can marry left- and right-brain activity, bring visual imagination to bear upon linear thinking.

Pictures matter. I regret that I was never taken into the countryside, knew no surroundings beyond the humdrum district of Liverpool where my memory kicked into action. My parents cared little for landscape or the natural world. But I had the garden, and there were picture books. To both, I trace the stirring of my visual aesthetic sense, my adult love of art. To that small garden I owe perhaps what sensitivity I can claim in the way of nature mysticism, a sense of the numinous. To one picture book in particular I can date my first religious knowledge (it was a book of Bible stories by Blanche Winder) and possibly, for the stories were finely told and held strong magic, my later religious inclinations.

Another vignette, a keyhole snapshot. My mother and I are sitting down to lunch. It is my favourite home-made pea soup, and I am eager for it. Yet obscurely I feel that there should be nourishment of another kind, that the meal should be dignified by some sort of theatrical embellishment. I go for the Bible story book. I open it at a favourite coloured picture of Ruth gleaning, her arms full of corn. I prop it open where we can both see it. Now the table setting is complete, the meal has the extra dimension it deserves. A notion: a liturgy, as I now perceive; a sacrament, blending body and soul in a whole experience, indivisible, satisfying.

# A CLUE

The first clue in the treasure hunt
is a taste of fruit.
'Of the tree of the knowledge of good and evil
if you eat, you die.'
Before we can identify the tree
we have sucked the bitter pulp.
Death? What death?
Is it death to walk the garden wide awake,
learning to know and name?
Out of hypnosis, Adam
cured of innocence
achieves promotion:
gardener, name-bestower.
Who would creep back behind the flaming sword
into a wombshaped paradisal crouch?
Neanderthal must square his shoulders now.

At five years old she knew the story well,
first in the picture book: the flaming sword
a rainbow marvel. Seraphim expel
Adam, stooping under a weight of word.
Knowledge of good and evil? Five years old
she could not know she had already heard
the black annunciation, had been told
at four-and-a-bit the painful difference.

The first clue in the treasure hunt
had been an ear at a keyhole.
That god her father
encountered unexpectedly one morning
eavesdropping, bending at the parlour door.

Within the room, that god her mother.
    'Daddy, what . . .'
    'Hush! I want to listen.'
Four-and-a-bit, she pattered back upstairs,
sick in a place that didn't feel like tummy,
equipped to recognise (years later)
the gargoyle called Contempt:
knowing that gods are clay.

## 2. Beyond the end of the street

Words, yes; pictures, yes; but no music. No child today could conceivably reach the age of five without hearing music, but such was my case. We had no musical instruments, no radio or record player (the 1930s terms were 'wireless' and 'gramophone'). My parents did not sing about the house and they were not churchgoers.

The excitement of my first day at school therefore was punctuated by two moments of sheer bewilderment. Turned out into the yard at playtime, the little girls formed a circle for a singing game. Whatever was going on? What strange noises were they making? I stood in the circle but not of it, astonished, uncomfortable. Then at the end of the short school day a hymn was sung. Again I stood ill at ease, uncomprehending, unable to disentangle words from the unfamiliar noises.

So to this day music remains mysterious to me, with singing more often than not only a way of obscuring words. Musical friends at various times in my life have exerted themselves to remedy my deficiency, but to little avail. I am beyond redemption. When others talk or write of music I recognise the vocabularies of artistic discourse but am unable to relate the words to their referent. It is a humiliating blind spot for one who loves the verbal and visual arts.

A flash-forward. Forty years after that five-year-old's amazement, I am at an Open University summer school. Attending a compulsory music seminar, in spite of having insisted that I am tone deaf, I am taken aside by the tutor, a distinguished London organist.

'Didn't you tell me you were tone deaf? You are not tone deaf, I know that for certain. Look, I wanted to congratulate you on your poetry reading last night. It was excellent – and it revealed to me that you know how to use pace, rhythm, pitch, modulation. Of course you are not tone deaf! Very few people are, you know.'

To gratify his curiosity, I stayed behind after class so that he could test me. Could I distinguish this note from that? The tutor tried several instruments. I failed the tests. He turned to the piano, running through variations on a theme. They all sounded alike to me, at least until he was contrasting one end of the keyboard with the other. The tutor admitted defeat, and began to question me about my childhood. I described the deprivations of a home without music.

'Very well,' he concluded, 'here is my diagnosis. You are not tone deaf but tone lazy – just as an optician might diagnose a lazy eye, organically sound but still unable to see properly.'

Music apart, I took to school with alacrity. It was mortifying, to be sure, to be given a card with my name on so that I could learn to write it. Did the teacher really suppose I couldn't already do that? It was, after all, such a short easy name: Anne Roe. A stubby, monosyllabic little name. I disliked it more and more as the years advanced. Anne Roe: two vowels, two consonants, it was spoken in an instant, before strangers could take it in. Then Roe was often spelt wrongly, with unwanted Ws here and there (Wroe, Rowe); and anyway proclaimed that I belonged to my father.

Reading and writing were pleasures, and school promoted them as such. It was a tiny Church of England school, once no doubt a village school, but now engulfed by the spread of Liverpool. There were three classrooms, three teachers: infants, juniors, seniors. My teacher, Miss Reid (or Read – for we were not given *her* name on a card) knew how to keep her children happy, though all at different stages. Being well ahead in reading, I (I alone, oh arrogant superiority!) was allowed to take down extra books from a reserved shelf and bury my head in stories while others struggled with writing or played in the Wendy house. Not until I reached grammar school would I encounter such congenial teaching. But

I was not long with Miss Reid, and my tears when suddenly uprooted for a quick family removal proved amply justified.

Outside, beyond home and school, a wild and wicked world awaited. My second experience of disillusionment was also my first encounter with crime. Some kind friend had given me a little secondhand scooter. It had red handlebars and a scuffed once-red footboard and was beyond my wildest dreams. No rich teenager with her pony, no flash young blade with his motorcycle, could be so thrilled and privileged. More, the scooter opened gates to the outdoor world – quite literally, for I was allowed for the first time to play in the street, unsupervised except for the older girl next door. Side streets in those days were safe for children, free of traffic except for the occasional delivery van. More often indeed, deliveries came on an errand boy's bicycle with basket, or even, still, by horse drawn cart. But traffic is not the only hazard. A small knot of children quickly gathered round the scooter, a high novelty.

'Give us a ride, give us a ride!' Unknown voices, unknown boys, bigger than me. Again I was bewildered. Longing to say no, I was helpless against the determination of the lad who seized my treasure.

'Only to the end of the street,' he shouted, pushing off skilfully. I watched in despair as he vanished rapidly from view, past the end of the street, out to the end of the world for all I knew. Devastated, I ran bawling into the house. There was never another scooter, not even a bike until I was twenty-one. Instead, I had stiff new knowledge in my armoury: people can let you down.

Meanwhile it seems my father was learning the same hard lesson. Remotely I knew that he worked in some connection with The Gypsum Company of Ireland, for there were pieces of gypsum on the mantelpiece, white angular chunks of a crystalline mineral. Father's boss, Carder by name, was I suppose a smooth talker. Genial and generous to us personally, he even paid for a few days in Llandudno, the only holiday I ever took with my parents. However, Carder was evidently involved in shady dealings. There was, as I pieced together later, an arrest, a court case, and offensive newspaper coverage citing my father as Carder's 'camp follower'. Since Carder had relieved the trusting Roe of all he possessed, the effect was catastrophic. House, furniture, ornaments, pottery, pictures, silver: everything had to be sold, and quickly. Taking only personal possessions, household linen and of course the precious books, we went into the first cheap furnished rooms my mother could find.

Though aware of her acute misery, I was too young to feel it for myself. And the first sight of our new abode, appalling to my mother, was intriguing if not comic to me. The accommodation was a so-called flat, the first floor of a shabby terraced house, with shared access to the landlady's kitchen. Its owner and sole occupant was a Miss Grimsditch, one of that extensive generation of spinsters with which the Britain of the 1930s and 1940s was populated. The war of 1914-18 had left an imbalance in the population, with many normally eligible women leading lonely lives.

Miss Grimsditch showed us upstairs. Two or three cats followed or preceded us. In the bedroom, two more cats lay luxuriously at ease upon the bed. In the bathroom, one peered from beside a pedestal. The feline stench, according to my mother's later descriptions, was overpowering. This was the beginning of many years, amounting to the rest of my parents' lives, of moving from unsatisfactory furnished rooms to others which, despite my mother's unquenchable optimism, always held hidden snags. I became used to setting out for school with an address carefully folded in my pocket, ready to go 'home' to wherever 'home' had moved to that day.

Some landladies were stern, unsympathetic to children. Some were generous, giving me clothing or teaching me (my mother certainly couldn't) to sew. Some had pets. I was made to take walks with a dog I rather feared and, unaccountably, collect a certain weed the dog enjoyed. A vegetarian dog . . . ? One had a parrot which could be taught a few words.

The joy of its colourful feathers and colourful language was seriously offset by the smell of its uncleaned cage. As for this first of our landladies, Miss Grimsditch kept open house to unlimited stray cats: sixteen at one count, but that was admittedly a high point. My task, soon explained and thereafter enforced, was to roll up scraps of silver paper diligently saved from chocolate or cheese (kitchen foil was still a generation away) and toss them for the cats to scramble after.

She cried, of course, when knees were grazed
or bad boys pinched and arms were bruised.
But that was only crying from the chest.
When sobs subside and sniffles fade
small tragedies are overlaid
and wounds redressed.

The new thing learnt from infant class
was how a storm of tears can pass
to a spectator's body, seize and strain
some intestinal neural band
as though the gut could understand
another's pain.

Sharp, localised above the groin:
our forebears said the bowels yearn.
Part pleasurable thrill, part prurience,
these tremors of the five year old
dismayed, attracted to behold
and deeply sense

the sobbing of another child. .
One's not so smoothly reconciled
to other people's tears as to one's own.
Awake that night, the child reverts
to those uncomprehended hurts
not quite her own.

She's scared of primal sympathy,
suspects herself of cruelty,
suffers the magnet pull of charity.
No man's an island, Donne declares.
The child, too vulnerable, shares
our solidarity.

## 3. Madame

What my mother thought of it all I am still unsure. Had she lived until I became a housewife, we might have discussed it woman to woman. Often distressed, she was always resilient. My father was in and out of work, more out than in, never sustaining any job for long. He was seventeen years her senior, growing visibly older with each disappointment, and dependent upon her in every way: emotionally, financially, for decision making. They never emerged from that sudden plunge into poverty.

But they were proud, intensely, absurdly proud. They were, I suppose – with few credentials for it – intellectual snobs. James Henry Roe, whatever his provenance, presented himself as a chartered accountant. He was not, and was frequently exposed as incompetent and sacked after a week or two at a job. Yet he continued to type, incompetently, letters of application full of false claims. He was determined never, never to be less than that to which he aspired. No doubt he could have done simple clerking, but the thought apparently was never entertained, much less that of anything more menial.

As for Emma Cleator, daughter of a Fleetwood gas manager, she had worked to become a professional woman. Her card and letterhead presented an impressive array of credentials, genuine in her case. She was LRAM (Eloc), LTCL (Eloc), MRST, Gold Medallist of the Poetry Society. These qualifications she flaunted. Emma wore – I do not at all exaggerate – patched rags for undergarments, she ate bread and dripping in order to feed me adequately, but never would she have considered doing any other work than what she always referred to as 'my own work, my profession'. She was the breadwinner until the end of their lives, and against the odds coped with financial problems more stringent even than I suspected at the time.

And it was true, she was professional. Not merely was Emma good at her job, which included a special expertise in Katie Thomas's breath control method by means of diaphragmatic grip. She was also an inspiring teacher and a superlative performer. How do I know what she was like as a teacher? Many an hour I spent discreetly hidden behind a screen in her hired studio, as she coached her pupils, usually adults, for Poetry Society or RADA. Emma was adored by her pupils. In later years a formidable presence in various organisations – the Women's International Friendship League, the Dickens Fellowship and others – she could quell a roomful of chattering people with that commanding voice: 'Ladies and gentlemen!' Associates in these gatherings and committees regarded her with something little short of awestruck worship.

She had the liveliest of blue eyes, set in a round face above a smallish nose. Upon that nose perched old-fashioned (even then) pince nez with a fine gold safety chain loosely looped to a wire-thin earpiece. It was a distinctive and distinguished feature. Possibly her most expressive feature, in that expressive actress's face, was her mouth. She had a way of upturning one end of it to express quizzical doubt, sardonic humour, or shared understanding. Mrs Roe in private, in public and professional arenas she was Madame Cleator, or simply and affectionately Madame. I loved her, I admired her, but did I know her well? I seldom confided in her.

Almost forty years after Madame's death, when I believed her forgotten by all but myself, I was startled and delighted to be proved wrong.

Barbara is a dear friend. I had known her for some fifteen years and we had both clocked up a sixth nought in the tally of our birthdays. In reminiscent mood one day, Barbara recalled how her elocution teacher had taught her to recite a certain poem. Some phrase, some intonation had a familiar ring. I questioned her.

'What was your teacher's name?'

'Oh, she was Madame. Madame Cleator. She was wonderful . . .' Barbara was off again, rattling away enthusiastically about the heroine and mentor who had taught her for seven years. When she paused for breath, I managed to tell her that Madame was my mother. The rejoinder amused me, and others present, not a little.

'Your mother? Madame Cleator was your mother? Never, how could she be, she was . . . she was *my* Madame Cleator!'

I was reminded of an incident when I was nine or ten years of age. A little friend at school, learning that I was Madame's daughter, was deeply impressed. 'What's it like,' she enquired, 'having a poetry mother?'

Then there was the Sunday School teacher who instructed me solemnly, 'You should go down on your knees every night and thank God for having given you such a remarkable mother.'

Yes, she was remarkable, larger than life, queenly. I grew up overshadowed, 'Madame's daughter', scarcely a person in my own right. Yet surprisingly I am not aware of having held that against her. On the contrary, I pitied her, tied, as I saw it, to that poor booby James Henry. When he dies, I vowed often to myself as I grew older, and I'm earning, I'll take her out and buy her the smart clothes she sighs for. I'll take her on holidays, we'll go to Stratford and the London theatres, I'll buy her books . . .

Mother too had her dreams, though I was seldom privy to them. One at least I knew about. On her bookshelves were ranged ranks of Everyman and World's Classics, bought in her London days, early hardback editions with yellowing pages. Notably, all the Greek dramatists were there in translation . . . awaiting her retirement.

'When I'm too old to go the library, I'll have them all to start on,' she explained, gloating fondly over the unread treasures. But even Madame was not in control of the fates.

Emma was born in 1899, into a lively family of whom she had many tales to tell, stories so remote from my own solitary childhood in a strictly nuclear family that they held the fascination of fiction. As well as an extended family (I heard for example of Great Aunt Ada Maria whose legacy at death was a large cabin trunk full, yes full, of white crochet cotton), Emma had a beloved younger brother and two somewhat older half-brothers. My grandfather's second wife died the year I was born, so he was my only known grandparent. In practical terms, he was my only relative, for we did not see the others, and it did not for a while occur to me to wonder why.

As a young girl, Emma suffered from a form of eczema in the hands, which became a convenient and lifelong excuse for not using them. She was clumsy with needle and kitchen implements, dropped and spilt things and made much of her ineptitude. My mother was not interested in housewifery. She would often joke that life in furnished rooms suited her well: instead of spring cleaning, just remove! Was this a defensive ploy to avert sympathy and sustain her own buoyancy? Partly, no doubt.

Problems at school over holding a pen meant that the teenage Emma was allowed hours to herself, left to read whatever she chose. What the little private school provided it is hard to imagine. Not paper qualifications, evidently, though perhaps encouragement to the girl's ambition. It left her at least convinced that free access to reading was the *sine qua non* of education. Accordingly, nothing on her own bookshelves was forbidden to me. Poetry was there in abundance, and 'reciters' treasuries' specially compiled for performers. Drama, of course: full length plays, one-acts, monologues. Shakespeare was king. All three of us had our own Complete Works, just as one had one's own Bible. Indeed Madame's Shakespeare, bound in black leather with gleaming gilt edges on the india-paper pages, looked and was treated like a beloved and often consulted holy book.

Emma might well have become one of those ubiquitous spinsters. She must have been fifteen when the First World War broke out, too young to have a regular boyfriend but part of a group of young friends. 'When the boys went' was a phrase that often figured in her tales of youth. Once, once only, I was allowed a glimpse of cards and letters tied with faded ribbon. The cards were delicately decorative greetings cards, some with lace edging and ribbon bows. 'From the boys out there,' she said. By the time she died, they had vanished.

When Emma was nineteen, some of the boys returned. By then, she would protest, she was busy, exerting every effort to liberate herself from Lancashire provincialism. The lights of London allured her, the great theatres, café society. Moreover, as she also admitted, in that postwar competition for surviving men she had little chance. Elegant as her clothes and deportment may have been, and when young she took pains, this was still 'fat Emma'. The later years on short commons made no difference to that. Her shape remained incorrigible, a lifelong sorrow to her. So much the greater, perhaps, was her achievement, that spellbinding quality, that magnetic personality.

# 4. The fist of fear

The skies are darkening. A great fist is clenching over Europe. Soon Neville Chamberlain will flutter his futile piece of paper for the newsreels. After that the digging will begin. Not fairies at the bottom of the garden but bolt holes, somewhere to cower when the fist closes.

A fist is a threat. A fist is also clenched in fear. Terror intensifies the grip, till fingernails drive painfully into sweaty palms. Europe is a fist of fear.

The grown-ups talk in low voices. Their faces are grave. Newspapers are studied with care. Small knots gather round neighbours' wireless sets. We children play as usual, but sense a menace in the air. Teachers sidetrack from lessons to tell us about the Great War. Here and there we catch words from our elders' conversations: 'trenches . . . gas . . . bombs . . . Poland . . . Herr Hitler . . .'

A man disengages from the earnest talk, looking down at me. 'Is she frightened?' he asks.

My father grips my hand firmly. 'She knows she's all right when she's with us,' he answers, reassuringly as he supposes. In fact he has just confirmed, and allowed me to admit to myself, that there is indeed something to fear.

Later, my father takes me for a walk. We are going as usual to the labour exchange and then to the public library where he will scan the job columns in the newspapers, for he is out of work again. But today we go further, for there is a marvel to be viewed. On a flat field in a Liverpool park is spread a thing of breathtaking beauty. Shiny sheets of silver silk, rippling a little in the breeze, spread far and wide for the sun to dance on.

It is a barrage balloon, someone tells us. No-one seems to know what it is for, but somehow it brings the horror nearer. How can such a dazzling delight occasion such unease?

And now it is happening, the thing the children have dreaded; but not, thanks be, to me. I watch from across the street, opposite my school, my closed school. They are taking the children away. Buses draw up like tumbrils. Mothers are crying. So is my own mother. I am not, I am selfishly happy, knowing that I do not have to be evacuated.

'Evacuated'. Emptied. The school is emptied, the city is emptied, homes are emptied. At the heart of the great fist is a hole, a hole in the heart.

For six years there will be emptyings: bomb craters, deaths, rationing, a hollowing out of lives to the mere simple shell of survival.

But lucky Anne is not evacuated. For some, the war is not all bad news. For those unfit to fight, there are jobs after the lean years. Arms manufacturers flourish. Vickers has opened a factory in Blackpool, and my father is to be one of the new work force. (The job didn't last, of course. He was sacked as usual.) So while other children are torn from their parents and taken to country or seaside safety, many indeed to Blackpool, my small family moves as a unit. I am eight years old and ready to start at a new school. Of late I have had lessons at home from my mother – English, history, anything else she could think of – and arithmetic with my father.

Schools are in difficulties: closed in Liverpool, filled to double their capacity in Blackpool. Teachers are uprooted, men to the war, women with evacuees. In Blackpool church halls are commandeered, just as all the guest houses are forcibly filled with either troops in training or evacuees. So 'we', the resident children (already I identify with Blackpool rather than with the incomers, even though I am writing maudlin verses about being in exile from Liverpool) take turns with evacuee classes to use school premises and equipment. Turn and turn about, mornings or afternoons are spent on hard benches in drab church halls. We have no desks, no equipment, no space, but there is always a piano. So we sing. 'Community songs', traditional ballads like My Bonnie Lies Over the Ocean or Ten Green Bottles constitute the only available fodder for young minds, it seems. I do not recall teachers even providing explanations of these sometimes mysterious ditties. The woman a-washing of her linen-O all week was comprehensible, washing machines being still unheard of, but who on earth were Bobby Shaftoe or Drake in his hammock?

Soon after these came a wave of patriotic songs, which our teachers encouraged us to sing with jingoistic fervour. In school, where maps were available, we were shown all that admirable pink around the world, the British Empire upon which the sun never set.

> The Empire too,
> We can depend on you.
> Surely you're proud,
> Shout it aloud,
> Britain's awake!

we yelled dutifully. Rule Britannia. For Britain, read England. England, it was impressed upon us, had never been beaten since 1066. England was invincible. England had an obvious and indisputable right to rule Scotland, Ireland, Wales, not to mention India, Canada, Australia, South Africa and much of the rest of the globe. Who if not the English had civilised and enlightened the 'natives' everywhere, transplanting cricket, parliaments, proper clothes and Bibles to benighted barbarians?

> There'll always be an England
> And England shall be free
> If England means as much to you
> As England means to me.

How our little bosoms swelled to those propaganda songs. How I cringe at the memory.

Early in the war gas masks were issued. Horrors of 1914-18 were still sharp in adult memories, though it was not until much later, reading Wilfred Owen's *Dulce et Decorum Est*, that I understood the terror. My own small fear is all I remember, standing in line in the school hall watching children ahead of me being fitted with their masks. In an instant ordinary girls and boys were being transmogrified into monsters out of nightmare. Then came my dreaded turn, the stifling of breath, the smell of rubber, the swimming sea-green scene beyond the visor. In minutes it was over and we could play again, as children do, easily shrugging off what is alien and incomprehensible, though at the same time committing it to long term memory.

Daily we carried the masks to and from school, out shopping, everywhere. Each had its awkward square cardboard box and shoulder string of coarse twine. Soon easier and more stylish modes of transporting the obligatory objects were invented, and a fashion market in slim colourful gas mask cases developed. As the gas scare faded, people became careless. Illegally, masks were left at home and finally forgotten. Oddly, the gas mask case fashion led to the shoulder-bag fashion for women, replacing the carried handbag. In days of severe clothes rationing, such fashion accessories became of pressing importance to young girls at puberty and adolescence. What else could you do, except adjust a hairstyle?

As gas masks faded from visibility, so did evacuees, leaking steadily back home. School resumed its normal tenor, give or take air raid warning drills. In Blackpool it was difficult to take the threat of bombing seriously, in spite of the Vickers factory offering a possible target. Nor, to my knowledge, were there more than two small bombs on the town during the entire six years of war. Anderson shelters had been dug in private gardens. Along the streets windowless brick and concrete huts were erected, into which you were supposed to dive if the warning sounded while you were out. No doubt these shelters would have collapsed on heads if a bomb had exploded anywhere near them. Teenagers, however, seemed to find uses for them. Emergency water tanks were set up here and there about town. Voluntary air raid wardens – my mother was one – organised neighbours into fire watching rotas and training in the use of stirrup pumps. These were simple water hoses operated from taps or the emergency tanks by the use of foot pumps. Water play with a stirrup pump was a coveted delight for any child who succeeded in gaining control of the pump at practice sessions.

Much has been made of the spirit of neighbourhood camaraderie engendered by the war. There is truth in this. Co-operation was absolutely required by the exigencies of fire-watching, shelter arrangements, rationing and the rest. But naturally this also threw up fierce feuds and resentments. It was a time of ragged nerves. There was black market profiteering and its righteous detractors, criticism of the unwilling and petty power struggles among the willing. We had better beware of nostalgia.

Central and local government were quite properly concerned for the safety of children. School had its air raid shelters at the end of the playground, and it was at first assumed that we would take refuge there as need arose. Air raid practice, like fire drill, was for us only an amusing diversion from lessons, a chance to race and jostle and squash. After a while, no incidents having occurred, we were told that anyone who could get home within twelve minutes would be allowed home if the alarm sirens sounded. Twelve minutes? Surely, even at 1940 speeds, attacking aircraft could travel a long way in that time. It is fortunate that we were never put to the test of a real raid.

By this time home had, as so often, been moved, so that my primary school was now some way away, a twenty minute walk in fact. Most children walked to school, for there was no traffic danger. The few privileged owners of private cars presumably locked them away for 'the duration', as petrol was only available for necessary commerce. I was therefore well used to my four times daily walk, and prepared to run if the alert signal was given. Could it be done in twelve minutes? The whole school was put to the test, each teacher timing each individual in her class. From school gates to home, a hasty parental signature to attest that we had made the complete journey, then back to school inside twenty-four minutes. Seldom have I run so hard, seldom been so disappointed. I did not qualify, and would have to stay at school in the event of an attack. On a second test run, however, I was allowed to go home with a little girl who lived close at hand. Rehearsals were a matter of much giggling as we squashed into the understairs cupboard designated as the family air raid shelter, and were given biscuits to eat by my friend's agreeable mother.

Party games, then, superficially. But we knew it mattered, we were truly afraid. Let oneself think, and the fist clenched hard inside.

T.S. Eliot postulated an 'objective correlative', a story or motif itself sufficiently charged with feeling to provide an adequate substitute on to which strong emotions may appropriately be transposed. By 1938 I was reading Kipling's *Jungle Books* for myself. Only now do I recognise just what my psyche was using them for.

## LETTING IN THE JUNGLE

They were looking at their watches
in Warsaw, in Berlin.
They were listening for the moment
when the shooting would begin.
   It is fear, O little hunter,
   said the nursery Jungle Book.
   They are letting in the jungle,
   Mowgli, look.

## The Girl Who Runs Backwards

The child was reading jungle tales
and sleeping at her ease.
Her elders, looking east, observed
the spread of a disease.
'Is she frightened?' asked a stranger.
'Not with us,' her father said.
It was only as he spoke she knew
presentiment of dread.
    It is fear, O little hunter,
    said the nursery Jungle Book,
    They are letting in the jungle,
    Mowgli, look.

They are letting in the jungle,
they are breaking down the fence
and chaos like the elephants
is trampling commonsense.
They are loosing Dionysos,
Lord Siva snaps the trees,
there is Logi in the forest
and St Vitus in the knees.
    It is fear, O little hunter,
    said the nursery Jungle Book.
    They are letting in the jungle,
    Mowgli, look.

Poland invaded,
Austria, France.
Hungary, Afghanistan.
The Vikings the Goths the Assyrians.
From the fury of the Norsemen
the burning of Troy
the sack of Rome
the last desecration of Zion
good Lord deliver.

*The fist of fear*

From letting in the jungle,
from clearing of the jungle,
from fruit of the tree of knowledge,
from nut of the tree of ignorance,
from pity and lack of pity,
from hurt of love and hurt of lovelessness,
from tug of root and tug of rootlessness,
good Lord deliver.

That the child may escape invasion
is a prayer for the woman's death.
Bring in the tribes, nomads and settlers,
bring in the banners the bugles the stamping hooves,
bring in the herdsmen grazing.
Bring in the dancers, the temple prostitutes,
the treble choristers – every new song:
war cry, town cry, far cry,
wolf and havoc and moon.

Announcing angel! regulate the invasions
but do not spare the child.
May she know a rose by the scent and the sudden fading,
the shapes the colours the velvet
and the sharp blood on her hand.
May she have eyes and ears
and a chronic hole in the heart.

## 5. *What do we know?*

This memoir is not intentionally fictional. Neither can it possibly be true. There are two reasons for that.

It has been said that the only accurate map would be a full size, 1:1 scale duplicate of the terrain with every detail delineated: an absurdity. Similarly the only true autobiography would need to describe every thought, action, experience and situation so fully that it would take a life to record a day. Worse than an absurdity, an impossibility, for to protect our sanity we are each equipped with an internal editor whose main duty is to discard excess luggage. Unfortunately we have little control over, and should have little trust in, that internal editor. It has its own agenda, and more dishonourable intentions than we suspect. Accordingly our memories are partial in both senses; and these are my two reasons for the necessary untruth of memoirs. We have usually been partial to our own interests as we unwittingly construct our recollections, and these are irritatingly partial in the sense of offering jigsaws with lost pieces.

That twelve-minutes-home regulation, for instance – was it truly twelve minutes or have I misremembered? When were gas masks issued? How long did evacuation last? If I were writing history I should have to delve into official and educational archives, discover what was decreed and when and by whom and for how long. But no, this is memoir. Rather like *1066 And All That*, it records what is memorable, in the form in which that quirkish internal editor sees fit to present it. Each of us is after all engaged upon a lifetime's project, to construct a story. Certain modern philosophers would have us believe that story-making is primary to human experience and integral to human consciousness. There is good evidence for it.

As for consciousness, that last unexplored territory which is baffling contemporary science in several disciplines, there are as we know layers of consciousness (sleep, dream, physical sensation, waking states, mystical states . . .) and also evolutionary grades. Consciousness differs through the animal kingdom, through human evolution, and through an individual's own unfolding awareness. Nor is this always straightforward. Kathleen Raine in her autobiographies describes retrograde periods in her life when she seemed absent from herself. I have suffered from similar episodes. It is as though the mind plunges into murky fog; or, to vary the metaphor, it floats idly upon the surface of the local pond, able only to address quotidian trivia. To emerge from such periods is a kind of awakening, a return to daylight and kinetic power.

My first sense of mental awakening, however, did not follow a time of withdrawal. It was merely the normal advance into that stage of human evolution denoted by higher reflexive consciousness. This, I suppose, usually occurs in the years before or around puberty. It brings two quite new capacities: for self-reflection or introspection, and for conceptual abstract thought. Not everyone notices the advent of these powers, but I did. In my tenth year I realised with profound excitement that I knew that I knew, I *felt* that I felt. About the same time I discovered the heady pleasures of ideas and generalisations.

This shift is often deplored in our personal and cosmic stories. We associate it with loss of innocence, as though it were a bad thing for Adam and Eve to become aware of themselves and able to manipulate ideas, instead of an exciting step forward. But it has to be admitted that as we mature there is loss as well as gain. Children feel intensely. Storms of tears, tantrums of rage, irrepressible laughter all proclaim it, while rational adults look on, wondering. The very young experience intensely, because the world is new and strange and worthy of attention, and their given duty is to explore it. These things we dimly remember in ourselves, or take care to forget. Poets must take care to remember, and not remember only but keep those sensitive pores open to continued stimulation.

There is a kind of heightened sensitivity which combines the directness of childhood sensation with the depth of reflexive consciousness. This combination is not easy to achieve, even less easy to sustain. Wordsworth sighed over the problem in the Ode on *Intimations of Immortality from Recollections of Early Childhood*. Aged nine, I could not of course have written this page, but I was certainly aware of the dilemma. Connecting it, correctly enough, with poetry, I coined my own term for this heightened awareness: 'the lyric thrill'. Most grown-ups, it seemed to me, had abandoned it. With great clarity the idea crystallized one day as I gazed at a patch of uncut grass.

## LONG GRASS

How can they all forget?
They don't remember, they don't want to remember.
Weren't they alive once?
Nine like me?
I shan't forget, I promise I'll remember.
Even when I'm forty.

She had climbed the fence on the railway bridge,
straddled the topmost wooden bar
and read the trespassers sign.

A grey town.
A terrace facing the railway
huddled meanly under soot:
two up, two down, no bathroom.
Goods wagons shunting.

*What do we know?*

The nearest tree a mile away,
the nearest field a world away.
Lawns she knew. Richer folk had lawns
and a bowling green was nearly as green as heaven.
She knew one, proudly.
But the railway embankment (London Midland Scottish,
Keep Out) had Real Grass.

Long grass, tall grass, feathers on the tip grass,
catch your breath and jump grass,
high as your waist.
Warm grass, sweet grass, suck it and taste grass,
summerful, bountiful,
Ceres and Persephone -
oh to jump!

They passed behind her, grown-ups from the shops,
and never even looked.
They didn't want to dive into long grass.
They didn't want to want to.
Why had they all forgotten?

Down in the grass you'd be secret from them all,
free like a fairy princess
rich under seedhead plumes
as though you had golden hair.
You'd belong to grass
and live its life and share its unconstraint
and peer between the stalks and see
through to the heart of things.

Even when I'm forty.
She set her chin
and set her alarm clock then and there
to ring when she was forty.

At forty she awoke,
spoke passionately again to long grass
(though she didn't want to jump),
recognised a rose by all its signs
and watched it turn transparent in her hand.


Around 1940 my mother was going through a bad patch. War news was gloomy. My father was unemployed and sinking into unemployability. She had few pupils and money was tight. So were the rations, not that she could have afforded much more had it been available. Unlike some, mother was not clever at conjuring meals out of scraps, and her culinary problems were compounded by the daily need for deft footwork when sharing a kitchen with the landlady.

There were clashes with the new landlady until a *modus vivendi* was worked out. One night a tempest of sobbing brought mother to my bedside, very surprised since I had not indulged in such a display for years. This, however, was to me a truly serious sorrow and worth vehement protest. I had been sent to bed as usual, but had been sitting up in bed writing a poem when Mrs Lewis, the landlady, had observed the light through the glass pane above my bedroom door. Angrily she ordered me to switch the light off at once and stop wasting electricity. I was forced to comply, but complained bitterly to my mother, sure that she would appreciate the high demands of the Muse. No doubt she had to pacify both me and Mrs Lewis. (I had better add that my juvenilia in fact showed no literary promise. I have long since decently destroyed all I wrote.)

We were, as it happened, unusually settled. From 1940 to 1946 we remained at the same address, the longest sojourn ever. It was the house with the parrot, and a landlady at least kind enough to let me play occasionally in the back garden. This boasted nothing at all except ill-kept grass and a (wickedly climbable) brick outhouse. I regret to report that my favourite ploys there were persuading ants to climb on to sticks –

however you turn the stick they insist on crawling underneath – and cutting earthworms in two for the pleasure of watching the two sections wriggle in different directions.

In spite of these deplorable juvenile pursuits, I was growing up fast, reading prodigiously and exercising my new-found mental capacities. Mother perhaps gave some impetus to all this. Her own low state required my promotion to adult understanding.

'You are nine now, and getting big enough for me to talk to.' This was a prelude to the relief of complaining, as it were woman to woman, about her circumstances. I see her now as she spoke those words, on her knees in a patched old dress, struggling to light the fire. A worn-down forty-year-old fat woman knelt there, bearing little resemblance to the urbane and scintillating Madame Cleator.

Another boost to mental development occurred about this time. An acquaintance of my mother asked permission to take me to Sunday School. Somewhat to my surprise I took to religion as to a congenial element. Here was the scope my new-fledged spiritual wings required. Here were ideas of real substance, indeed of cosmic significance. And here was language, the rich Jacobean English of the Authorised Version. I was enchanted.

According to the teachings of these Methodists, God was an invisible person, present everywhere, to whom one could speak directly. He – for this anthropomorphised being was of course male – was in the business of improving us morally and of guiding us into whatever situation he had planned for us. He was luminous and beautiful beyond imagination, and we could love as well as worship him. It was probably easier to love him if you addressed him as Jesus. There was the word Father, but that didn't appeal much to Anne.

I became for a short while an extremely pious child, though secretly,

35

for I was aware that one must observe the social decencies. In the privacy of my bedroom I compiled, in a notebook I quaintly entitled 'A child's book of religion', a sort of commonplace book of Beautiful Thoughts and prayers. Kneeling conventionally at my bedside, eyes ardently closed, I addressed that benevolent deity and expected him to speak to me. Hardly surprisingly, he did. Little psychology is required to explain the ensuing phenomenon.

It was a vision. As I knelt in adoration, eyes closed, I seemed to be kneeling before a desk or table on which were writing materials, with a vacant chair on my side. Though I 'heard' no voice, I was aware of an absolute imperative: 'You must write.' Whatever part of my psyche was addressing my consciousness, its message was unmistakable. Oddly enough – or perhaps not so odd, for it happened at the next highly sensitive age in my development – I experienced precisely the same vision at age fifteen. Never at any other time in my life have I seen visions.

What do we know? How do we know the world, each other, ourselves? How do we tell ourselves that which we need to know but dare not know? How do we use our myths, our stories, our beliefs and rituals, our language and art, in this unending exploration into understanding? And are we, as ironic self-aware postmodernists, possibly moving into a further stage in the evolution of consciousness? If so, New Age freaks could have a point. If not, the outlook for humankind is bleak.

> For the pure in heart alone
> the beatific sight.
> To Bernadette and Joan
> that given, oblique light,
> that lady by the spring,
> those voices calling.

To be agile on the climbing frame of reason,
athletic with abstract concepts,

to shuffle and deal and fan ideas
with the sophistication of bridge-players:
these are the marks of maturity.
Who, after all, would be Bernadette or Joan?
Visions were old-time magic lantern shows,
tricks played on a peasant imagination
by a peasant subconscious.
There may, we concede, be that which transcends reason,
but pictures are only for children.

> When that oblique beam
> transects the brain's arc
> only the simple dream
> of pictures in the dark.
> Simpletons then,
> Bernadette and Joan.

A sprinkle of home psychology explains it:
projections on a low-level screen.
Why posit announcing angels?
But the force, authority, absolute command,
the numinous pressure?
That unrepeatable unsolicited givenness,
fear that is also joy
and lifelong jet-thrust of imperative?

Pure in heart? Hardly,
but this was no epiphany of godhead.
Pure in heart? No.
Simpleton, perhaps.
Twice to the growing girl the plain picture,
the same wordless bidding.
The child could neither formulate nor compass
that solemn fiat;
the woman would not stoop to pictograms.

The only possible twice
somewhere between.
Thin enough the mental ice
at ten, fifteen,
for images to break
out of the lake.

Table, paper, pen,
a gaping chair
extorting the amen
of Mary's fearful prayer:
accepted motherhood
half understood.

## 6. *Myths have meanings*

It is common for small children to invent imaginary playmates. When this happens, the child presents every appearance of believing in the actual existence of the invisible companion. It was not so with me. My imagined other did not emerge until I had crossed that frontier of consciousness already described. I was nine or ten years old and fully self aware. I knew quite clearly what was pretend and what was not. Yet I felt the need to create an alter ego or subordinate sister, one who would listen to my stories, admire my poems, share my fantasies and aspirations. She was called Angela, a name significantly similar to my own. The great advantage of Angela was that, unlike real-life friends, she never got tired of listening to me and never contradicted. She may not have lasted more than a year; at least I cannot recall taking her to grammar school.

About this time I became aware, among other things, that I was an only child. It didn't trouble me. Indeed it was clear to me that an only child gets all the favours and treats, while at the same time avoiding sibling rivalries and squabbles. This seemed an admirable arrangement, and if there were deficiencies Angela supplied them. But I did wonder why there were no sisters or brothers. Questioned, my mother was evasive and defensive. It hadn't seemed a good idea. We hadn't much money. My father was older than most. None of these reasons rang true. I felt sure she was lying.

Then one day I believed I had the answer. I had idly picked up the newspaper. My eye lit upon an article about illegitimate children, a category hitherto unknown to me. How they came to be illegitimate was still obscure, but it certainly involved some secrecy and doubt about parenthood. At once I leapt to the obvious conclusion. So *that* was why my father was so uncongenial to me, so unsuitable in age and every other way to be either my mother's spouse or my father. I was pleased, mentally cheering and dancing. He was not my father! It must have been someone else, someone doubtless clever and splendid enough for my mother but for some reason unable to marry her. And James Henry Roe, who loved my mother (that I never disputed) had adopted me. I had just reasoned my way to this satisfactory conclusion when my mother, in some embarrassment, snatched the paper from me, thereby confirming my guesswork. Not daring to raise the matter with her, I hugged my hope in silence.

Already I had discovered that before moving to Liverpool we had lived in Preston. There were even photographs to prove it. But before the photographs? It was permissible to ask where I was born. The slightly surprising answer was 'in a Blackpool nursing home'. And was I christened? Oh yes, at some church near Preston; here my mother became vague. Why was I given my middle name? I was Anne Watson Roe. Again she was evasive. 'Some people we knew then, friends of ours called Watson.' She hurried away, obviously eager to put a stop to the questioning. So now, I believed, I had the whole story. Certainly we had no acquaintances called Watson. *Ergo*, it was the name of my real father. One day I might discover more, but this would do for now. Problem solved. And so I lived happily ever after, that is for the next fifteen years, with this false concoction of a story. It was hardly more real than Angela.

Human beings tell themselves stories, then believe them. The tales may not be true, but there is always a reason for the telling, and the truth is in the reason. I am fascinated by myth. The Dream Time, the infancy of human consciousness, throws up stories by which the tribe lives, identifies itself and makes sense of the world. Later, more sophisticated ages at first reject the tales as untruths, then begin to appreciate the significance they carry. And so the tales are recycled – by a Euripides, a Racine, a Joyce, a Freud, indeed by countless poets, artists and taletellers including myself. We feed on that ever-renewable nourishment the myth-makers provided. Something of this was revealed to me at nine and ten, as part of that marvellous mental leap.

I loved the old stories: Greek, Norse, Judaic, Celtic. My books had children's versions of them. But it was not until the age of ten, precisely the ripe age for it, that I made the thrilling discovery:myths have meanings!

My mother – no, this is not a digression – was not a practical woman. Thrifty she had to be, but it was not in her nature. She had self-control, strong as steel whenever it suited her, which was most of the time. Indeed, the power to exercise self-control, whether in technical breathing functions or emotional self-discipline, was the virtue she most often enjoined on her daughter. Mother also allowed control to lapse when it suited her, and whether that was wisdom or folly is arguable. If this particular day's action was folly, its effect was that of a far-seeing wisdom.

Clothes could be patched. Shoes could be mended; my father had lasts, cobbler's tools and offcuts of leather with which he repaired all our shoes himself until the uppers crumbled. But eventually even my mother had to have new shoes. She saved the money, a little each week from 'the housekeeping', and now she set out for the .shops. Later in the day she returned, having bought no shoes. Instead, smiling defiantly, she unwrapped her purchase: a book. The lesson in priorities was not lost on me.

The book was *Myths and Legends of Greece and Rome* by H.A. Guerber, a fine illustrated edition with plates showing famous paintings and sculptures. No children's book, this, but a popular study for adult readers. I pored over it, story after story, picture after picture, re-reading. Then one day, feeling I knew every tale in the book, it occurred to me to read what looked like rather a dry chapter about the origin and meaning of myths. Great windows opened inside my head. Myths had meanings! They spoke of sky and earth and sea, of dawn and fire and vegetation, of love and war and death. A lifelong curiosity was awakened.

## MYTHS HAVE MEANINGS

Guerber unbricked a wall in the child's head,
let in adulthood.

Myths have meanings.
The play had been enthralling, but now this!
The stage backcloth, a pastoral scene with willows,
hillside and stream suggested, subtly lit,
was drawn up, abruptly.
Backstage, no theatre wall . . .
the Alps in daylight, waterfalls and wings.
She blinked, and stepped outside.
Raphael, Botticelli, Milton, Keats
waited to take her hand.
Plato, Bultmann beckoned her to climb.

Past every alp, a higher alp.
From certain climbs you may descend again
by other routes, using another rope,
reaching a different base.
If myths have meanings, meanings may need myths.
Minds that mean the meanings make the myths.
Homo sapiens needs his story time
and all his coloured pictures.

Myths have meanings.
Bo-Peep goes skipping, glad to lose her sheep.
Meanings pull their myths.
Mary, go and call the cattle home.

Oedipus, Dionysus, chthonic powers,
we claim your savage masks.

*Myths have meanings*

Diagnosing evil, we must name
Eve, Adam, Lucifer.
Crying for mercy and a purer way
we cling to carpenter and fishermen,
bread, and a bag of nails.

* * * * * * *

There are the tinsel myths
lighting on Christmas trees
to sparkle children's mornings:
sky song, star and hay,
frankincense and lambs.
      Tinsel, even for adults
      retains defensible
      magnetic properties.

There are the iron myths
that nail and rivet us,
all too believable:
screaming turbulent mob,
convenience politicians,
clandestine arrest
for fear the cock crow.
      Iron pulls its weight
      provides retaining anchors;
      hammers are so familiar.

There are the amber myths
to cure the king's evils,
like rubbing for a genie:
walking calmed water,
multiplying bread,

43

breaking from a tomb
and paralytics leaping.
>The attraction in the amber
>(health in honied glass)
>lures with electric charge.

And there is a gold myth,
a dream of alchemy.
Being transfigured before them
his face shone as the sun,
garments white as light.
Lord, it is good to be here.
Peter, bathed in gold,
babbles delirium.
By the tree of golden apples
they saw him as he was.
>This was the alchemy that tugged a child:
>to glimpse divinity under the tall grass,
>to look through a rose window
>towards the Hesperides.

# 7. Food, books and John Alfred

Food, glorious food, is probably the first joy in infancy. Because we are animals, food remains central and vital. Because we are human, it has become much more than mere sustenance. Our species has developed food varieties and combinations galore. To gustatory and olfactory satisfactions we add a whole range of others: aesthetic pleasure in colour and texture; social enjoyment as we eat with others; the ceremonial marking of special occasions; associations with surroundings such as dining rooms, restaurants, picnic places.

I love food. I enjoy planning meals, I take pleasure in shopping and stirring, boiling and baking, setting a pretty table and presenting colourful dishes. I like to ply guests with the plenty I so seldom enjoyed as a child. Yet I also retain a streak of puritan asceticism, a preference part of the time for plain simple fare and a game-like pleasure in making-do, creating meals from Hubbardish cupboards. There is no consistency in all this, unless in the likelihood that both attitudes derive from the sharp hungers of childhood.

For what with the war and my mother's lack of money and skill, I was often necessarily hungry. There is no virtue in that, but it did at least teach me to value and actively enjoy what food was available. And there was always enough somehow, especially at Christmas. Before the war there would be a tangerine and a sugar mouse in my Christmas stocking, along with small sundries such as a pencil, a handkerchief, a hair ribbon. Christmas dinner was usually roast beef or roast pork, and even wartime rationing seemed to allow for that. Many families would have a celebratory chicken but, odd as it seems now, chicken was then a luxury more expensive than prime beef and beyond my mother's purse. There would be Christmas pudding. Even in wartime sufficient dried fruit could be saved towards the pudding-stirring, and eked out with carrot, suet and flour. The white sauce for it (rum? – not in our teetotal household) would be made with dried milk, a precious scrape of butter and a rare spoonful of sugar.

As for the tangerine in the stocking, such exotica were no longer available; but by now I had grown beyond the hanging of stockings. Christmas meant books. If there were other presents I do not remember them and will not have valued them at the time. Only the books mattered. We were a family of readers, all three of us. An occasional card game might be played, but on the whole our united opinion was that leisure was *for* reading. I joined the public library on my ninth birthday, the very first day the regulations allowed, and became an almost daily borrower. I delighted in the sight and feel of those solid, thick hardbacked books, their alphabetical arrangement, the deft quick fingers of the librarian as she flicked through trays of tickets. Perhaps, I pondered, one day I could do that. One could do worse than become a librarian.

My taste was deplorable. To be sure, I was at the same time reading steadily through the good literature on the home bookshelves, but from the library I borrowed schoolgirl stories by Angela Brazil and her like. My mother viewed with impatient disapproval this regular diet of pap, but with wise forbearance did not forbid it, knowing that the fever would burn out eventually, And after all the Angela Brazil *genre* was to little girls what the novelette is to women. Under the veneer of some glamorous location – in this case a snobbish private boarding school – is explored that interplay of personality and relationship which is the human female's immemorial concern. They have their place, these trashy tales; they at least begin to teach young readers how people live together.

But the craze was obsessional. My first Christmas after joining the Guides, some half dozen of us went with our Guider on Christmas morning to visit the local orphanage, taking toys and books we had collected. Very shy, we gathered in a huddle at the door of.the orphanage playroom, unwilling to cross the threshold although strongly encouraged by Matron. Then one of us observed the bookcase.

## Food, books and John Alfred

'Just look at their Angela Brazils! Oh, the lucky things!'

All dutiful pity for the plight of the poor orphans vanished. So did our shyness. We surged in a body towards the bookcase, where shelf upon shelf was filled with our favourite author.

Brazil was followed, in my case, by Louisa M. Alcott, then John Buchan, Jeffrey Farnol (fustian historical romances) and finally a year's diet of detective fiction. By that time I was thirteen and ready to abjure the rubbish. To my mother's wry relief, from then on I read real books.

From earliest years, Christmas morning meant a heap of books. Some were from my mother's pupils and friends. One, always, was from my grandfather, and this was special. With it each year until I was eight came a long letter, read aloud by my mother because I could not decipher my grandfather's handwriting. The letter narrated at length and in spellbinding detail grandpa's amazing adventures in search of Father Christmas, from whose hands he had personally received the book. Each year the journey was different: through the air in pursuit of flying reindeer, over snowy wastes, surviving hairbreadth escapes. It did not matter that I ceased to believe in Father Christmas after I was five. My grandfather could spin a yarn. The only time he ever stayed with us I had magical bedtime stories every night.

In fact it was only in my secondary school years that I came to know him better. By that time John Alfred Cleator, retired gas manager, erstwhile Methodist local preacher, was in his eighties and almost totally deaf. He used an old-time hearing aid with a very large battery prominently situated in a waistcoat pocket. This he would ostentatiously switch off if a speaker bored him, a fairly sure conversation stopper. Long widowed, John Alfred was looked after by his assiduous housekeeper Annie, whose most vital function was to have meals on the table promptly. John Alfred too loved his food. His hearty cry of 'Tuck in! Tuck in!' was music to my young ears; how different from my mother's 'No more just now.'

47

Dinner at grandfather's Fleetwood home was a seriously substantial affair taken at midday. The main course had to be followed by a pudding and pie. 'Pudding' meant a milk concoction of rice, tapioca or sago. 'Pie' denoted a top crust over a deep dish of stewed fruit. Well do I remember one woeful occasion when pudding appeared unaccompanied by pie, and the terrible thunder of John Alfred's preacher's voice as he roared for the culprit.

'Annie! There's NO PIE!'

Happily for Annie and all at table, in fact there was a pie and the omission was rectified with proper contrition.

Annie's cooking was done in and on the ancient gas cooker which had been state-of-the-art when her employer had headed the gas company in Fleetwood. She supplemented its deficiencies by using the old black-leaded open range, so that there was always a black iron kettle on the fire and often a black iron stewpan. Beside the fire, on the hob, were socks.

John Alfred had become obsessed with socks. He insisted he had sweaty feet and must take care not to take cold. It followed, apparently, that socks must be changed twice during the course of a day. The socks were very long, stocking length, very thick and made of pure wool, so the drying process was a matter of constant anxiety.

Together with the antique cooker, the gas lighting was of strictly historical interest. All the ground floor rooms had gas mantles to which a match was carefully applied while with the other hand the lamplighter pulled a small chain. I was never permitted to perform this sensitive operation, for a clumsy move would wreck the flimsy mantle, and the insertion of a replacement was a task requiring skill and delicacy. As for the rest of the house, a rambling three-storey building with staircases in various directions, there was no form of illumination. You took a candlestick from the hall table, casting flickering shadows on stairs and passages. Arriving in a bedroom, you placed your candlestick on the marble washstand, beside the ewer, basin and soap dish. These were made of pottery (first floor) or enamel (second floor). It was a house frozen somewhere in the 19th century. Even the ironing was done by gas, with two heavy irons, actually made of iron, which were heated by standing over a gas flame rather like a bunsen burner, one being reheated while the other was in use.

The front parlour, slightly darkened according to genteel custom with lace curtains and the obligatory aspidistra, was seldom used. I tried with little success to picture it animated by throngs of relatives and friends as in my mother's youth. Occasionally I would wander in there, not daring to dent or crumple the stiff black velvet cushions, hand painted with moonlight scenes. A glass fronted bookcase held the preacher's stock in trade, 19th century books of sermons and biblical commentaries.

By the time I was cognisant of his reading habits, John Alfred had set all that aside. He still read his Bible daily after lunch, sometimes dropping asleep over it. Otherwise, in his eighties John Alfred had become a devotee of the detective novel, especially the works of Agatha Christie. He insisted on pronouncing her Agaytha, accent on the second syllable. Because his short term memory was failing and he could not bear not to think back over books recently returned to the library, my grandfather kept meticulous lists. Under the title and author of each thriller appeared the names of detectives, victims and all the suspects. Any failure to provide himself with this reference tool would leave him driven distracted, with the hapless Annie dispatched to the library to make the necessary enquiries.

In the middle parlour lived Miss Clarice Cleator, John Alfred's sister. She was a formidable lady, tall and firmly erect, stern of aspect. Aunt Clarice gave the impression of one who minds her own business and hoped very much that we would do likewise. She gave piano lessons, so the efforts of her pupils could often be heard. This did not of course impinge upon the deaf John Alfred. There was, I think, little fraternisation between brother and sister.

Upstairs, in a remote back room, lived an even more reclusive female, a Miss Scragg. I glimpsed her only twice, but she seemed aptly named: wild of eye, strange of demeanour, with tufts of dishevelled white hair starting from her head in all directions. Miss Scragg had evidently once been a friend of Miss Clarice Cleator but had by now lost both health and wits.

My grandfather died when I was fifteen. I was not at the funeral. I have no idea what became of the house or of the two women. Life is littered with unfinished stories.

# 8. Reading and Guiding

Whilst my grandfather had settled down to Agaytha, my mother was reading largely biography and travel – together of course with what used to be grandly termed *belles lettres*, namely poetry, drama, essays and 'good' fiction. Her tastes were on the whole middlebrow, though she would wince to hear me say so. My mother would distinguish, anyway, between her run of the mill leisure reading and literature to be taken seriously.

Second only to Shakespeare in the parental pantheon was Dickens. For perhaps the last fifteen years of their lives my parents were pillars of the Dickens Fellowship. Though I never saw my father actually read a Dickens novel, mother was intimate with almost the whole *oeuvre*. She owned a complete set, which occupied a full shelf of my father's home-made bookcases.

These bookcases constituted all the furniture we owned, and were duly moved from furnished rooms to furnished rooms at least eight times. My father was proud of his handiwork, and lovingly stained and polished the thin cheap planks from time to time. How mortified he would have been had he seen the inventory made after his death of the pitiful household chattels! Those precious bookcases were dismissively described as 'painted wooden racks'.

That was the time (I was twenty-five) when in the aftermath of my parents' deaths I donated the set of Dickens to the Dickens Fellowship. The local secretary and his wife, to whom I took it, were shocked. To them it seemed sacrilegiously disrespectful to Madame's memory that I should so easily shed her treasures. But I had heard Dickens read, rehearsed, recited year upon year and grown heartily sick of him. My mother made her own abstracts for recitals (she would no more permit the demeaning word 'recitation' than I would allow 'poetess'). The

51

highlight and climax of each year's syllabus at the local Dickens Fellowship was 'Madame's night'. This consisted of some two hours of recitals; no readings from the book, every word was memorised. By careful editing of the text mother produced dramatic monologues and duologues, often – as with her Shakespeare recitals and others – performing two roles herself. Other subsidiary voices were allowed. My father was coached in the men's parts, I in the children's or young women's. Some years her star pupils were enlisted to perform. Though Madame presented fresh material every year, certain favourites were often requested by the Fellowship. In particular, her rendering of the tense scene between Miss Pross and Madame Defarge (*A Tale of Two Cities*) never failed to thrill the audience. For light relief, Sairey Gamp (*Martin Chuzzlewit*) offered a vehicle for the elocutionist's comic genius at its most uproarious.

So I had had enough of Dickens by the time I left home. In middle age I repented and began to read and re-read him, a pleasure perhaps the keener for its delay. Unlike the rebellious teenager who resented having Dickens thrust upon her, the grey-haired woman was equipped to appreciate that author's marvellous artistry in language, the wit, even the grotesquerie.

It surprises me a little now (for we take much for granted when young) that my mother never seemed to read politics, philosophy or religion. These subjects were not discussed, though as to religion, for the last ten or more years of their lives both my parents regularly attended a Methodist church. Their political ideas were probably rudimentary, based on unexamined assumptions picked up from The *Daily Telegraph*. My mother was the founder and first president of something called The Women's International Friendship League, but this was hardly political. Its aims were based on a generalised humanitarian concern and focused on the prejudices generated or exacerbated by the war.

A *caveat* is in order here. Members of large families can to an extent check their childhood memories by comparing notes. I have no such recourse. Statements about the presumed attitudes of parents who died forty years ago must be made with uncertainty and received with suspicion.

Try as I will, I can recollect no overt ethical teaching by my parents, though I have an impression, which I cannot substantiate, of having received by osmosis some notion of standards of behaviour. Only those exhortations to self-control – not a very positive moral value – are clear in memory. Yet I did have some wish to be 'a good girl' and knew that goodness, whatever that is, was expected of me.

It was when I joined the Guides, at about eleven, that systematic moral instruction reached me, in the form of the Promise and the Guide Law. To these teachings I pinned my amorphous aspirations, and was glad enough even a quarter of a century later, as a Guider, to pass them on to a new generation. Yet another quarter-century beyond that, and I have some reservations.

The Promise was, my Guiders impressed upon me, the most solemn I would make that side of my wedding day. I cannot claim to have honoured either set of vows, but at least the Guide Promise provided guidelines for life.

The wording in those days was
>            I promise on my honour to do my best
>            to do my duty to God and the King,
>            to help other people at all times
>            and to obey the Guide Law.

As for the ten demanding rubrics of the Law, we were taught an abbreviated mnemonic. A Guide must be
>            Trusty, loyal, useful,
>            sisterly, courteous, kind,
>            obedient, smiling, thrifty
>            and pure as the whistling wind.

The mysterious last line referred to a Law equally mysterious to us children.

'A Guide is pure in thought, word and deed.' I suppose it was an Edwardian periphrasis enjoining us not to think about sex. The promises to God and the King proved equally slippery. The second, in 1942, could be easily construed as patriotism and doing one's bit for the war effort. Later, duty to the Queen was interpreted as good citizenship and taking an interest in the Commonwealth. Duty to God meant going to Sunday School, reading the Bible and being, vaguely, a good girl. Possibly it included all the other promises anyway. Oddly, it seemed to have nothing at all to do with religious experience, awe of the holy, the mind aflame, my 'lyric thrill'.

And so I made the Promise in eleven-year-old good faith, and remained a Guide until nearly sixteen. Guiding was good for me. It offered what home could not and school did not, a sisterhood of children of varying ages. With Guides I learned practical homecraft skills which would never otherwise have interested me. With Guides I discovered that singing can actually be fun. With Guides I first sampled the unknown delights of outdoors and the countryside.

Almost as soon as I joined, our Captain was snatched away into the Land Army. From then on we were with difficulty provided with a series of temporary Guiders from the WAAF (Women's Auxiliary Air Force) in transit training in Blackpool. There was no possibility of organising camp holidays until 1945. That summer, as part of the 'dig for victory' effort, some of us went not on holiday but to a pea-picking camp. Through the day we laboured – oh, hard work it was! – in the pea fields, but in the evenings there were camp fires and the thrill of sleeping under canvas. I was by this time a patrol leader and in charge of a tent of seven girls. My system of bedtime discipline worked perfectly: I read them ghost stories. Every night, exhausted from field labour, the girls dropped to sleep before the end of the story and begged to hear the dénouement retold the following morning.

It was while we were at this camp, at a farm near Skelmersdale in Lancashire, that the war reached its final conclusion, VJ Day. That morning we were on our way through country lanes to the pea field when we met two WAAFs and an airman.

'The war's over!' they shouted jubilantly.

Our leaders dispatched runners to the village for confirmation. Yes, it was true. Work was abandoned for the day and we returned to camp. The farmer made a barn available, and our elders set to work to provide the wherewithal for a party. How and where they obtained provisions I never knew, but a great feast was held, followed by party games well past our bedtime. As darkness fell we could see fireworks and searchlights over Liverpool. Oh frabjous day!

Guiding encourages creativity. For me only one kind of creation was conceivable. I was going to be a writer. Between the ages of ten and fifteen my most passionate hopes, indeed expectations, centred on that ambition. After all, had not my 'vision' – a secret divulged to no-one – confirmed it as a high and holy vocation? So sheet after sheet, notebook after notebook, was filled with execrable verse, feeble short stories, stilted playlets, pretentious essays. It is well that we cannot foresee our disappointments. That weight would be too heavy for the young.

# ZIGZAG BRIDGE

Curious how, looking back, it's *things* you see.
People are worn out dolls with faces gone
or turned surrealist: trunks with sunflower heads.
Things can remain.
               A wall we used to climb
where different levels tested our attainment.
The child who fought for footholds with me there
melts to a hairslide and a skipping rope.

And near the wall, that footbridge. Zigzag Bridge.
It measured and enlarged us. Such an age
to do the zigzag up on roller skates,
but zigzag down was bliss. And on the top,
lords of the railway, colonists of heaven,
we tugged at freedom like a rising kite.

By Zigzag Bridge we crossed the railway line
into a territory of otherness
where grown-ups wandered freely. Outer space.
The margins of infinity. We knew
that Zigzag Bridge was magic. We could feel
the start of possibility, the end
of leading strings and nursery certainties.
We grew on Zigzag Bridge. It was immense.
Such steps! Such steep inclines! Such long approaches!

It's smaller now. Is that because I've grown
and crossed all kinds of bridges – some to come?
Rather, I feel diminished, bridge and I
cut down to size together now the dares
and jumping games are over.

Zigzag Bridge,
everything's to and fro and up and down
this side the railway, here in grown-up land.
People get faceless faster, too. Even things
don't last like you did. Nothing's quite so huge.

## 9. Freedom and spending power

Imagine, if you can, the carriageway of Blackpool promenade devoid of traffic. There are trams on the tramlines, pedestrians on the seaside broadwalk and the inland pavement, but on the road only a few pushbikes. Gaze as far as the eye can see along that straight stretch of South Promenade, and it is as though the internal combustion engine had never been invented. Today, an environmentalist's dream; yet this was often the scene during the Second World War. There had indeed been vehicles before that, in the 1930s, but from my own first memories of Blackpool they are absent.

It followed that in spite of the limitations of war we children enjoyed a freedom unknown to any generation since and unimaginable today. 'Playing out' held almost no dangers for us, for parents almost no anxiety. We, and they, knew nothing then of violence or child abuse. It was a strangely innocent time, in spite of the atrocities being perpetrated around the world.

So we roamed at will. In Liverpool I had had the run of a park across the road. In Blackpool, eight and older, my friends and I visited each other's houses at considerable distances, walked lengthily to school, took off on roller skates for breathless whirlings on the broad promenade areas. My skates were inferior quality and left me unable to catch up with better equipped children. That was part of being poor, as later was my secondhand old-fashioned tennis racket. It didn't matter. A bicycle was out of the question, but roller skates had wheels of a sort and wheels were freedom. The human animal has this urge to transcend its physical capabilities. We devise wheels, sails, balloons, wings. We construct mythologies of angels. Neither apes nor angels, we ape the angels.

There was, to be sure, the blackout. It only affected me as I grew old enough to go out after dark, usually to Guides. Blackout was strictly enforced. Every window had to be covered in black before switching on a light, and stern were the reprimands for any householder showing a chink of light when the warden passed. Walking out on moonless nights required care and skill. You carried a pocket torch, the beam of which had to be directed downwards to the feet, never aloft.

Growing up with this, we children took it as a matter of course. How intense then the glory, the fairytale freedom when, the war over, street lights were lit again! Here indeed was the 'lyric thrill'. Not merely the eyes but the spirit exulted. To look up at trees underlit by street lamps, their leaves golden and translucent, was as heady a visual excitement as sunset over the Jungfrau. I was by then fourteen, then fifteen, sixteen, possibly the optimum age for religious awe; the lamps lit me. This may seem a bizarre idolatry, to worship street lamps. Not so. Whatever enlarges the lungs of the spirit to their uttermost, allowing us to breathe the air of heaven, that thing is holy. All places, all times may be sacramental. Just about the time the lamps were lit – 'the lights are going on all over Europe' was the popular phrase at the time – Edith Sitwell's poetry enjoyed its brief season of esteem. Enchanted, I memorised the lines beginning

> Old people at evening sitting in the doorways
> See in a broken window of the slum
> The burning bush reflected.

There are burning bushes everywhere. I hope the young are still seeing them. I am.

For all our blessed freedom, then as always poverty restricted excursions. My parents almost never took me out except for dull walks along the promenade. Pocket money was minimal. My very first, very daring request for a penny for a Milky Way was received with surprise, but the request granted. I was eight, and after that received a 'Saturday penny' for some time. This I would usually spend on halfpenny pencils and twopenny notebooks. The amount rose to threepence, then to sixpence by about the age of ten, though there were weeks when it did not materialise at all. With sixpence, serious money, one could take a tram ride into town and prowl the shops. Woolworths, then 'the threepenny and sixpenny store', was a Mecca for stationery supplies and the coveted coloured hair-slides. With fourpence to spend, I could indulge my dream of gluttony, an apple tart from a cheap snack bar. For by this time the penny and twopenny chocolate bars on sale early in the war years were removed from children's reach by rationing. My mother would buy a bar of chocolate once a month and portion it out between the three of us in single small cubes.

The tuck shop next door to my secondary school had little tuck to offer by 1942. I could not afford to patronise it anyway, but would unashamedly hang around in the hope of falling in with a friend with money in her pocket. Then we would purchase a bag of parched peas. These were dried peas, cooked and overcooked until black and very salty. Today's children with their salty crisps are enjoying a similar pleasure, though it is not so rare a treat to most of them. An adjacent bakery, usually displaying little but empty shelves, had no fancy cakes to tempt us; but if anyone had money she would buy a malt loaf which, lacking butter, we would simply tear into chunks to assuage those schoolgirl appetites.

If you have to be poor, it is best to be poor in wartime. Others may have more, do more, but not so very much more. Clothing was rationed, travel restricted, holidays abroad out of the question. All our glamorous dreams were concentrated on the cinema, everyone's escape hatch. Birthday treats were visits to the pictures. Any extra windfalls of pocket money were spent in this way. When I was thirteen there was a craze for collecting pictures of film stars. Betty Grable, leggy, busty, blonde, was the idol of the moment. I went to one of her films, realised – to my mother's satisfaction – what rubbish it was, and reverted to books. At this point I was testing a fresh freedom, freedom from peer group culture. None of us ever altogether escapes it. But that judgment I set over against the mindless film star cult – was that my own, or was I merely substituting my mother's values? No human is fully autonomous. No schoolgirl is an island, to paraphrase Donne. Yet surely we are each responsible for weighing and evaluating?

But I did have a yearning for pretty clothes. Most of my dresses (trousers were not then worn by girls) were charitable donations of some sort. They seldom fitted, they were never chosen. I knew better than to complain. My mother's struggles to fit me out in secondhand uniform for Guides and then for grammar school were all too evident. Or rather, not always evident to me, for many years later a school secretary sorting out old files showed me a letter from my mother to the headmistress. It was a begging letter, requesting free cast-off school uniform for me. I had not known that she had ever been reduced to begging. My so-proud mother, the eminent Madame Cleator: whatever did it cost her to write that letter?

Throughout the war the national make-do-and-mend campaign encouraged dressmaking. This was beyond my mother. She hated needlework and had much ado to keep up with the never-empty basket of mending: socks to darn, underwear to patch. Her sewing was clumsy and owed too much to Great Aunt Ada Maria's coarse hard crochet cottons. However, mother did rather enjoy trimming hats. Hats were worn by both sexes on all occasions, and as my mother could not buy new she would ring the changes with feathers, ribbon, artificial flowers. Her drawers still held hints of 1920s elegance. There were multi-coloured taffeta scarves, long silk gloves that reached to the elbow, a parasol, and the last tattered remains of rose-trimmed *crepe-de-chine* petticoats. At home in the mornings she wore the customary housewife's printed cotton overall. For afternoon and evening wear, especially in public, she contrived to have one or two decent dresses, being careful never to raise her arms lest the darns or patches in the armpits be exposed.

I, having almost no clothes but school ones, fantasised. Newsagents sold pattern books, illustrated selection catalogues for dressmaking patterns. When a new edition arrived, I could often get a superseded one free or for threepence, and would pore over it avidly. At thirteen, I did actually acquire a pattern and ineptly set about constructing a blouse.

My mother looked on in amazement. 'Is this my daughter, sewing?' she marvelled. I could not decide whether her expressed admiration was genuine or sardonic. The blouse proved unwearable. Since then I have been no great needlewoman myself, though not without some interest in the art; but at thirteen I probably needed ways of being something other than Madame's daughter. It was doubtless part of growing into freedom.

## *FLYING*

If it were not for birds
how could we have concocted
that dream of air?
So effortless! – as though
from tree to ridge tile were
a step any one of us might take today
or at least tomorrow.

If it were not for hawks
and upside down blue tits
and of course butterflies
and admittedly the wasps
we wouldn't be Icarus
with all those nightmares, daydreams,
gliders and star wars.

How do they, why do they make it look so easy?
Did angels – I mean those strong rebellious ones –
equip these fliers to contradict the earth,

set up a counter creation?
If it were not for wings
we shouldn't resent our feet.

If it were not for flight
maybe we wouldn't – knowing
how in the end we have to lie down flat –
project our fantasies of afterlife
as heavenly aerobatics.

# 10. Honesty

Since my retirement I have become a Quaker, the logical culmination of a lifetime's quest; or so it seems to me now, for we must never claim to have arrived. All that is required of a Quaker, ethically, is to live simply, peaceably, honestly. (All!) But to acquire honesty, that is a dance of the seven veils; and the veils are not seven but seventy times seven. Probably this memoir is part of the dance.

I may thank, or blame, the Guides for first articulating for me this impossible aspiration.

>I promise on my honour . . .
>A Guide's honour is to be trusted . . .

These were concepts bigger than I knew. Trivial benchmarks were provided: you kept your promises, you returned from an errand with all the change, you owned up to naughtiness. But concepts of honour and honesty go deeper than that. They have to do with both integrity and understanding.

For my twelfth birthday, my parents gave me (what else?) my very own Shakespeare, which I still use. They inscribed it with a quotation from *Hamlet*, selected I know with much deliberation.

>To thine own self be true.

At twelve, I was not sure what that meant or where it would lead me. It has taken the rest of my life to work it out. On the way it has shattered my marriage, governed my choice of work, directed my thinking.

The young may have innocence but not yet integrity. Only experience provides enough material to integrate into a whole person; not that any of us achieve final wholeness. Similarly the young may have directness but not yet understanding. To be honest with oneself demands discernment. Intellectual understanding helps. I can now, for instance, interpret my

64

'vision' because I have read fairly widely in psychology of religion. More difficult and more vital, though, is that deeper self-knowledge acquired through interaction with others. It is a painful process, peeling off layer after layer of illusion and self-deception.

So my Girl Guide years were only the beginning of this arduous quest. Nor was it merely a matter of growing up. Adolescence may be the worst time for the would-be honest. Certainly adolescents are acutely self-aware, self conscious and self centred in every sense of those overused phrases. But it is a period when the growing human, reaching out to the world, is vulnerable to whatever presents itself. To rebel, in those years, is to conform. Visit any high school on its non-uniform day and you will observe an entire population in blue jeans.

The young must have excitement. Whether what they encounter be drugs, alcohol, sex, crime, loud music, political or environmental campaigning, terrorism or fundamentalist religion, if it is bold and brassy and provides the kicks they crave, that is what they will adopt. They cannot know that for this they are trading integrity, honesty, clarity. Indeed, if challenged they will affirm vehemently that they are at last truly honest. At that stage, I fell victim to evangelical religion.

There are other, subtler pressures, the pressures not of youthful peer groups but of the whole society. Today the most obvious is consumerism, our shopping-oriented culture. In the 1940s and 50s it was a postwar social reaction, the return to conventional marriage-and-home, that held sway for young women. At that further stage, I fell victim to the social requirement for a wedding ring.

But I move too fast. First came the grammar school years. Here my memories become sharp and detailed, for I very consciously revelled in secondary school life. Equally consciously, I set it over against home life, where poverty and lack of opportunity were making my parents ill and unhappy. Increasingly I felt choked at home, only alive when retreating inside myself to read or write, or when out at school, at Guides, with friends. So my memories of home at this period are accordingly blurred. How honest can I be, at this distance, about those home circumstances and about my own feelings?

The Blackpool Collegiate School for Girls was a 1920s red brick building. Its two wings stretched along two streets at a right angle, with ample playing field space behind. Between the two extended wings rose an imposing central unit accommodating the entrance hall, assembly hall, headmistress's room and sixth form suite. This centrepiece was approached by a broad flight of steps leading to a Greek-style façade with Ionic columns. Every child in her first year would learn in ancient history lessons about the modes of classical architecture, Doric, Ionic and Corinthian, and be urged to admire the grandeur of our own school frontage. (It is all demolished now. A block of flats occupies the site.) Thus simply and without spelling it out, teachers connected our own academic institution with the sources of western culture. My already awakened enthusiasm for the Greeks was quickened. It was a disappointment that we did not learn Greek, and cause of resentment that the boys' grammar school did offer that privilege.

## SEVEN SWANS FOR HELLAS

'You were born in Greece,'
a travel poster said.
Europa's children, all
Hellas bred

on the Acropolis
meet ourselves at home,
recognise that light's
nursely welcome.

Apollo, sun and song,
gold of lyre and hair,
clarifies our sight
on lucent air.

Round Leto's island swam
seven sacred swans;
seven circuits made
for her defence.

On the seventh day
his most holy birth:
Apollo, sun and song
shed on earth.

Swan escorted god
heralded by seven
fit for Leda's love
(Mary's, even)

your annunciation
signs our history.
Sing, but never swansong,
lest Hellas die.

Seven swans for Apollo.
Seven signs: the bow,
the shepherd's crook, the sun car,
the laurel on the brow,
the python and the tripod,
the athlete's form and face,
insignia of a seven branched
intellectual grace.

Seven swans for Hellas
where conception starts.
White wings over Europe,
double seven arts:
word and shape and number,
discus, column, mask,
measuring rod and healer's wand,
shards for voting cask.

Angel of announcements,
speak our mother tongue,
Greek-rooted syllables
heard when we were young.
Set us new assignments
using Homer's speech:
myth making, mind waking
Icarus' reach.

Joy in words, that other civilising ingredient from my home nurturing, was also encouraged by the school, and not only in English lessons. Other languages opened fresh delights. French, Spanish, Latin revealed not only the fascination of other speech sounds but also revealed exciting kinships among words, intricate chains linking culture with culture. I never acquired enough Latin to read Latin authors, and at the time it seemed the most useless subject on the syllabus. Yet for the rest of my life I have been grateful for that basic smattering of Latin which has allowed me to understand English words as I could never otherwise have done. Arguably it has in fact proved the most useful of all my school lessons.

Extra-curricular activities reinforced pleasure in language: drama, a writer's circle, a debating society, essay competitions, French oral competitions. Never for a moment did it occur to me to feel, as my son unhappily did at his school a generation later, that oh! so English anti-intellectual shame about loving words and books.

The debates about grammar schools and single sex schools persist. I have heard all the arguments, and hold no strong opinions. To have enjoyed my own schooldays gives me no mandate to prescribe for others. We were 'selected' at eleven, then within the school selected again by streaming. Perhaps we did grow up in a thoroughly unnatural and unhealthy ghetto. One age, one sex, the academic top stream – was it a very narrow world? In some ways it was. Knowing no boys allowed me to leave school fearful of one half of the human race, regarding the male of the species as both alien and barbaric. Mixing only with the academically able reinforced that intellectual snobbery my parents had unwittingly inculcated. Honesty – since that is what I am pursuing here – compels me to admit that I have never fully liberated myself from those two objectionable taints; even though my intellectual aspirations were never realised and even though I have since discovered that some men are human!

There were other aspects of school life to which I did not take so readily. Each year a singing competition was held, for junior and senior choirs of the four so-called school 'houses'. Participation was compulsory. For weeks, everyone was forced to attend singing practice until the two songs were rehearsed to perfection. On the day itself the songs were heard four times over and the winning choirs selected. At an early stage I found myself released from this bondage. Prowling round the circle of singers, the music teacher seized upon me and commanded me to be quiet. Very willingly I stopped singing.

'You are not to sing again, you put everyone else off,' she admonished me.

This allowed me to absent myself from all future choir practice. On the day of the competition I sat with some half dozen similarly undesirable non-singers – out of a school of six hundred. I felt not shame but gleeful pleasure.

Sport likewise had no allure for me, though the school encouraged it. My school reports however bear an unvarying 'Satisfactory' from the PE teachers. This is no doubt because they did not recognise the name of this unknown child. I soon learned how to play truant from PE and games sessions. Every cranny in that building capable of hiding a reluctant pupil was known to me. There were dressing rooms beside the stage, technicians' workrooms behind the labs, certain downstairs cloakrooms seldom supervised; there was even a manhole cover in the music room floor through which, holding a torch, one might descend into obscurity.

Never once were these absences pursued or discovered. But on the single occasion I truanted from an academic lesson, luck was against me. It was an afternoon of extreme heat, and the prospect of a Latin lesson did not appeal. Margaret, who was top in Latin, and I who was second, deserted to the shade of the 'wood', a mere copse at the end of the playing fields. In that wood as first-years we had built romantic secret bowers of woven twigs. Now at fourteen we sought its shelter in hot weather for interminable discussions on Life The Universe And Everything. Carrying our Latin books, then, we took cover. Quickly Margaret and I prepared the exercise we knew the class would spend the lesson struggling over; then we lay back lazily. Almost at once a familiar voice reached us. The teacher too had deemed it a day to be outdoors. She had led the class out on to the field, but soon the heat had become overpowering and they also made their way to the wood. There was no escape, short of jumping over a wall into the street. We were caught.

For our teacher, a nicely balanced dilemma. Should she punish us for so deceitfully absconding, or should she commend our scholastic diligence in having already correctly completed the afternoon's task? We had been, you could say, honourable in our dishonesty.

Life is peppered with honourable dishonesties. Every kindly white lie is one such. The document I am now writing is another. I have acknowledged the impossibility of truth telling and of objectivity. I cannot vouch for my motives in writing. And yet this whole effort is directed towards more honest understanding. Reader, be as indulgent as my Latin teacher! She let us off, and listened to us.

## *HONESTY*

Alone is when you kick off shoes,
scratch, fart, pray, sing out of tune,
address the garden spade by name.
Luxuries of alone.
Ha! got you, honesty, caught you!
I'll keep you now
pinned under my clothes.

It's not a safety pin.

Set a garden chair out in the sun.
Read for an hour.
How did the shadow line net you?
Honesty is like that.

Place a cat on the hearthrug.
Insolently
she mounts your seat,
stands on the chairback,
deftly flicks her tail
along your neck.
Honesty is like that.

Clean windows with brush and leather and cloth
and three buckets of water.
Watch that sunshine.
Streaks are worse than rainspots you erased.
Honesty fails again.

Alone is when you don't use printed fabric.
Genuine embroidery: there's a luxury.
Alone is when you tidy out a drawer
of mixed embroidery silks.
Trouble's tomorrow.
Hooligans break in, tip out all the drawers,
tangle your skeins,
mix up all your motives.
Vandals made away with it, then, did they,
that honesty?

Alone is when you come home from the play,
mock their ham posturing
but suddenly notice
you're wearing motley.
Honesty, walking shadow.

Alone is when you're Socrates to self.
Socrates didn't blink
though hemlock got him nowhere.

*Honesty*

Even at the end, though, Crito still
blinked with astonishment.
The rest of us have only Crito's way
to ordinary deaths,
dusty, dishonest.

# 11. A woman's place?

A senior mistress at our school told her girls that the teaching profession no longer boasted eccentrics such as those she remembered from her own youth. The gale of laughter that greeted this remark disconcerted her. Our generation was particularly well blest with eccentrics, in our view. We ascribed this to their being old maids, members of the brave brigade of surplus spinsters who staffed schools and hospitals in the mid-century.

One of our Latin teachers will serve as example. She sang and danced as she repeated the declensions and conjugations we needed to memorise. *Hic, haec, hoc* took her prancing across the room; with *hunc, hanc, hoc* she capered back again. '*Fenestra*, window!' she shouted, touching a pane of glass, then plunging rapidly to the opposite wall pointed up at a small window. '*Fenestrella*, little window.' Then, in dramatically heightened tones of endearment, 'Dear little window.' Finally, flouncing away in simulated disgust, 'Potty little window!'

One day she strode into the classroom and without a word began to write on the blackboard. On and on she wrote, as we waited and wondered. It appeared to be a nine-lined poem in Latin, incomprehensible. The teacher put down her chalk and turned.

'Now, girls, sing. Sing that.'

We stared in amazement. Surely our mad mistress had crossed the final border into insanity? Then she began to sing. Raggedly, we caught on. The song was a generation out of date but we knew it: *Daisy, Daisy*. Word by difficult word, she took us through the Latin paraphrase, in which the 'bicycle made for two' became a species of light war chariot. I still have the whole thing by heart. To conclude, she explained the punning word *tandem*, Latin for 'at length'. Though I have forgotten the teacher's name, she would be gratified to know that her lessons are so well remembered half a century later.

I know now that this was not eccentricity but good teaching. For women at that time the teaching profession provided enviable scope. In spite of the number of men away at the war, women had not yet reached far up the hierarchies of other professions. Girls' schools and women's colleges, like hospitals, provided an accepted arena for bright women to reach positions of authority. By the 1940s those surplus single women were of an age to take command, as head teachers or hospital matrons for instance, unencumbered by the difficulties of maternity leave and childcare.

It was rather different for the generation which came to maturity after World War Two. That war left no such extreme imbalance between the sexes as had the first, possibly because there were so many civilian casualties. When the men returned, however, those women who had taken their places on the land, in the factories, in shops and offices, were expected gradually but gracefully to vacate their positions. Such feminism as had survived the earlier suffragette fervour and been carried comfortably though not militantly by the spinster generation seemed almost extinguished in the 1950s. The *mores* of the time required of a woman that she seize a man, marry correctly and conventionally, put on a frilled apron and subside into domesticity. People today find it hard to believe that when I married in 1957, although I was a fully qualified librarian, I was obliged to leave the profession. Local government allowed no married women on staffs of town halls or libraries; or at least the government local to me.

To return, then, to my secondary school years. A mild, optimistic, taken-for-granted feminism prevailed as the school ethos. When the debating society suggested the apparently incontrovertible proposition 'This house believes that women are equal to men' it seemed impossible to find a speaker for the opposition. Daringly I accepted the challenge, and in the event carried the day by arguing that on all counts except muscle power women were indubitably superior.

Life at the Collegiate School was rich in such activities and societies. Indeed our form was often singled out for comment by teachers as a class whose initiative exceeded even the school's high expectations. In our first year we maintained a regular form newspaper on our classroom wall. As third years we set up clubs for tennis, rowing, writing, arts and hobbies. In the fifth form we distinguished ourselves by staging a mannequin parade, first for the school and later for parents and public. The parade demonstrated all the items of school uniform, showing how they should and should not be worn. The obligatory school hat, for instance, was modelled as worn in varying styles from years one to six. These hats were soft 'pork pie' shapes, squashy and malleable, the basis for limitless schoolgirl creativity. Since shortly before this I had written and produced a fifth form play, it fell to me to write the rhyming commentary and as *commère* to speak it from the platform while my classmates performed. It followed therefore that I was also required to be spokesperson when a journalist from the local paper telephoned for details of the event.

Summoned by the school secretary, I made my way in trepidation to the office. The telephone was handed to me. Taken by surprise, I struggled to answer the reporter's questions, squirming inwardly with alarm and embarrassment, for the headmistress sat implacably beside me listening.

'So tell me,' continued the cheery pressman, 'are you yourself wearing correct school uniform?'

'Er . . . well, not exactly.'

'Describe to me what you're wearing.'

Would nothing distract the head's attention? Miserably I mumbled my way through a description. Blue blouse, should have been white. Royal blue skirt, should have been navy. Wrong stockings, wrong shoes. As I faltered through the incriminating catalogue the headmistress's gaze followed stitch by stitch. I knew what to expect when the interview ended.

76

It didn't come. Not a word of reproach. I escaped relieved but puzzled. What was going on?

This was autumn 1946. The war was over, but clothing was still rationed. Knowing that I would have to leave school at sixteen, my mother had equipped me for my final year by using clothing coupons, not to mention money, on non-uniform clothes in which I could go out to work the following year. If a *fait accompli* were presented, she reasoned, the school could do nothing about it.

Meanwhile my headmistress was concerned with more important issues. Mrs Robinson (for she was by now married, this being evidently permitted to schoolteachers though not to other local government workers) must earlier have been the recipient of that parental begging letter and knew something of our circumstances. By this time she had met Madame Cleator at public functions and knew her also as a friendly acquaintance. I wonder how she reconciled the two *personae*? I can scarcely do so myself. When my intention to leave at sixteen was signalled, Mrs Robinson went into battle. Anne would, she assured my mother, be certain of an Oxford scholarship. There were ways of funding a student. It would be wicked to withdraw her from formal education. She stressed the child's talents and prowess. She even showed my mother a confidential document. It was the list of pupils who had passed the eleven-plus examination in 1942, in order of IQ rating. My name apparently figured first.

Nothing prevailed. I pushed away the thought of leaving, too proud and too distressed to reveal my heartbreak at school, and half believing that it couldn't happen. Some *deus ex machina*, some knight in armour, would at the last minute rescue me. But poverty was not the only reason my parents proffered, and against their other argument Mrs Robinson and I were helpless.

Some two years previously, my mother and I sat one afternoon in a cinema. When the house lights went up at the interval, mother remarked casually, 'Oh, look at the time!'

'Look where?' I asked.
'The clock.'
'What clock?'
'There, just to the right of the screen.'
'I can't see any clock.'

When we emerged blinking into the afternoon sun, my alarmed parent marched me at once to an optician. 'Test this child!' I still recall her imperious tones.

Yes, I was shortsighted, with rapidly deteriorating vision. When I got my glasses the world was remade. Astonishments ambushed me at every turn, delights of detail freshly perceived. How long had my sight been failing? How much I must have missed! Buildings and interiors, trees and grass sparkled in unimagined clarity. Colours were suddenly intense. There were burning bushes everywhere. I moved in a glory, treading holy ground. Thirty years later that heady experience was almost repeated, when with my newly acquired hearing aid I switched on to birdsong. Such sensations are not just analogues of divinity; they are truly religious experiences.

## AMBUSH

Yes.
It almost seems like loitering with intent.
The ambush set, at every corner waits
the sharp shock of a changed horizon, gates
swing open to reveal a new disguise.

78

In what strange semblance he'll invade your eyes
there is no preconception, till dilates
some close familiar thing with alien weights
of beauty, and the crouching seagulls rise,
crying and swerving in astonishment.
     High rise
     surprise
     equates
     ascension with assent.
Yes.

But vision was a problem. My lenses were changed, at first, about every six months. My mother became anxious enough about my failing sight to consult a specialist. The consultant was reassuring. I would not go blind, the rate of deterioration would decrease. However, responding to mother's impassioned questions, he agreed that too much reading should be avoided, adding the advice to get outdoors more. My mother's anxiety was certainly genuine, and it seemed to her that higher education was out of the question. Yet in the event my studies were to be at least as arduous, my reading hours at least as prolonged, as I would have faced at sixth form and university.

I shall never know to what extent the eyesight argument was a rationalisation. Finances were desperate. My father would never work again, my mother earned little. She could teach only intermittently, needing to spend much time caring for the ailing James Henry. In spite of our frugal lifestyle, I think she was desperate. There were drains on the family purse of which I was still ignorant. The prospect of supporting me for a further two years' schooling seemed unthinkable, even if Mrs Robinson were correct in her hopes of university grants afterwards.

I had always been accustomed to accepting the exigencies of poverty, and behaved accordingly. I hid my resentment and heartbreak. But did I give a thought to my mother's? Had she not shown me a cherished book of etchings of Oxford colleges, conveying with it something of her own unrealised dreams? What was her disappointment and chagrin at having to snatch away her daughter's chance of the glittering prizes? This I cannot know. Too well, perhaps, she had learned and taught those lessons in self-control. Instead of weeping together, mother and daughter concealed their feelings from each other.

Would it have been any different had I been a boy? I cannot help speculating, though my parents gave me no reason to do so, and most of my female classmates went on to sixth form and beyond. Yet the social climate was changing, the postwar reaction towards feminine domesticity was perhaps already starting. Even the anti-domestic fiercely professional Madame was beginning to hint to me that the security of a marital home was every girl's desire. The picture she evoked was of 'a real home', a phrase she used significantly often, with a husband as provider of the security she never enjoyed. Had she survived to the 1970s and the new wave of feminism, would her attitude have changed?

# 12. Marrow jam and narrow friendships

Letter writing is a dying art. I regret this. Telephone conversations with friends are companionable; they have immediacy and the reciprocity of dialogue. Fine. But I miss that quickening of the heart at the handwritten envelope on the doormat; I miss the reading and re-reading, the keeping and years-after discovering. Once a frequent letter writer, I miss the scope no telephone talk can allow: enough time to think, to choose words, to narrate or reflect without interruption. But then I was an early apprentice.

In a wartime effort to develop in the young some international understanding – travel being impossible, and a siege mentality dangerously limiting – pen-friendships were encouraged. Schools and youth groups facilitated them. At one time I was enthusiastically writing to unseen pen-pals in Scotland, France, Spain, Australia and the USA. Most of my correspondents tired of the exercise before I did, though I think it was I who terminated relations with the Spaniard. He was older than me, already at university, and had published his first slim volume of verses. It was entitled *Adolescent Anguish* (I translate literally) and the contents were woefully appropriate.

My American friend lived in Manhattan. Her family owned a limousine and a yacht; there were holiday snapshots of her glamorously clad figure on this vessel. Little wonder she wearied of the dull doings of an impecunious Lancashire lass. But at least there was the food parcel. Long promised, and awaited with mounting suspense, its final arrival after who knows what Atlantic delays was a high day, a day of marvels. Tinned peaches! Corned beef! White pastry mix! All were gloated over, then hoarded for Christmas to supplement our rations.

Rations were of two kinds. 'The rations' were prescribed amounts of foodstuffs considered basic, such as tea, butter, sugar, bacon. Other groceries were 'on points', so that the shopper could choose, say, either a jar of jam or a tin of Spam. This name was a contraction of 'spiced ham'. Speck or suspicion of ham would be nearer the mark. Eggs and milk came in the form of dry powders. Bread there was, flour there was, but of one sorry sort. 'National bread' was made of the only flour available, a kind of dirty grey and tasting of nothing. Lacking butter, it could be spread with dripping, for what meat we could get was fatty and every drop of liquid fat from the cooking was strained and kept for use. Shortly after the war, when a friend of mine married, her mother gave her a basin of this home-made dripping as the first and in her view most essential item for a bride's stock cupboard.

With dripping, chips could be made. The only party ever contrived for me during the war was a chip-and-pea party. This took place one day when the landlady was away. My mother cooked batch after batch of chips and passed them through the kitchen window to an eager queue of children, with mushy peas cooked from soaked dried peas. It was a great success with my classmates. On the strength of that party my personal stock rose and I ranked high in the pecking order until it was forgotten.

A national Dig for Victory campaign made greengroceries fairly plentiful, though restricted to whatever could be grown in the local area. Environmentalists, applaud! Potatoes, cabbage, carrots and lettuce were cheap even by our standards. At Collegiate small allotments were made available where we could grow our own produce – not that my horticultural ambitions soared beyond radishes. The school's Anderson shelters, half raised above ground like ancient burial mounds, provided on their sloping sides strips which we could cultivate. Meanwhile the school cooks, rather more productive, raised cabbages and vegetable marrows outside the dining hall.

Secondary schools provided hot dinners, though in my first term I had to make do with a daily packed lunch until a free pass could be issued. This was always meat paste or fish paste sandwiches, my mother being either unable to afford or unable to invent alternatives. Lower School dinners came ready cooked in metal canisters from a central town kitchen. They were usually uneatable after this method of transport, but of course we ate. I developed a technique of closing my eyes on lumpy custard as I swallowed it and thinking of strawberries. This must have had its difficulties, as I think I had only twice tasted strawberries, but at least allowed imagination full play. Upper School dinners, cooked on the premises, were more palatable – except that those assiduously cultivated marrows allowed the cooks to ruin every pudding with marrow jam.

Each table of ten girls was an entity. Since all portions had to be eaten, and this rule was firmly enforced, syndicates were formed. One girl would dispose of seven portions of the fatty gristly meat on which most of us gagged. I would accept any number of servings of cabbage, usually eight. Being always hungry, I would likewise account for any unwanted puddings, bolting them at speed in order to be in the queue for second helpings. Questions were asked in biology class about the likely effect of this on Anne's internal organs. The teacher predicted dire digestive troubles at forty. I have lived to prove her wrong.

'After the war . . . after the war . . .' was the burden of everybody's longing, adults and children. Often the expressed wish was for a food item. Butter, bacon, bananas, oranges, chocolate were mentioned. The mother of a schoolfriend vowed that her first postwar luxury would be a Battenburg or Neapolitan cake, pink and yellow sponge layers coated in marzipan.

Such food fantasies were evidently a way of expressing the deep dissatisfactions of the time and of focusing wistful hopes on a golden age to come. 'After the war' had some hallmarks of the past, as seen in rose-lensed nostalgia. 'In peacetime we had . . .' was the phrase which partnered 'after the war'. Britain was to return, not to the soup kitchens and unemployment of the 1930s, but to a mythical world of harmony and plenty. Politicians and intelligentsia may even then have been agonising over the economic conundrums ahead, but the people at large preserved a naive faith in a future stable and serene.

Of course it wasn't like that. Rationing persisted, there were urgent housing problems. Men with physical and psychological problems returned to estranged families and difficult job seeking. The cohesive effort that had upheld British morale snapped. There was, I suppose, a national identity crisis. Had we really won the war?

And there were as yet inconceivable changes to come. New technologies would change lifestyles, communications, the very way the world views itself. Sexual mores would alter, generation gaps widen, global eco-problems become apparent. In the never-had-it-so-good sixties, Alvin Toffler published his chilling *Future Shock*, forecasting how the very pace of change itself would accelerate.

Into this unlikely shifting world I grew up. But my own identity problems were more immediate than those of the nation, for to be young is to be inventing oneself. The young have to be self-absorbed. I am glad I need not endure adolescence again. And yet . . . are we ever as mature, as relaxed, as confident as we pretend, or do most of us remain adolescent at heart?

# *WILD HORSES*

Who would be young? The rapture and the terror –
where pins are swords, a frown lays bare a skull,
where sobs and fists are used and usable,
where any step bananas into error,

cut shins, confusion; every wall's a mirror
for blushes . . . then a dancer's sudden twirl
giddy with grandeur: joy expendable,
coinage for profligates and more to spare.
The old don't feel like that. The old are wise
and calm and confident and clear and cold.
They know the ropes, have packed a toothbrush, means
of access or of exit.
                                    Craven lies!
Come, blow that gaff! Brag how the frenzied old
seize in the salt Camargue those streaming manes.

Our primate relatives live in groups. That is their survival strategy. Unlike bees, termites or fish, primate groups are composed of animals with brains evolved enough for individual consciousness. Hence the necessary cohesion of the group depends upon the skills of living together. In other primates we can observe the beginnings of complex human emotions: loyalty and betrayal, concern and outrage, the fondlings of affection and the frenzies of jealousy.

Humans are still grappling with all this. Clever toolmakers, we are poor fumbling learners in the social skills we so urgently need for survival.
                    We must love one another or die
as Auden wrote, starkly. In our species it is mainly the females who shoulder this burden. Girl, woman and crone, at all ages we interest ourselves in relationships. Schools provide a limited close group, unnatural in its age limitations, but still a surrogate tribe in which to practise our skills. Girls' schools especially are forcing-houses, particularly perhaps for those who like me have no extended family.

Do you remember the wet days of your childhood, the dive-for-cover and better-stay-indoors days? I scarcely do, though there were plenty of them. I was not an open air enthusiast, being very definitely non-athletic, yet surprisingly my more vivid memories of schooldays are of outdoor huddles with classmates. I travelled to secondary school by tram. These trams were not the streamlined beauties of Blackpool promenade, but ancient double-decker bone-shakers on a now vanished inland route. They had perilous staircases and coveted wooden seats in the open at each end of the upper deck. Here friends would gather, careless of the Blackpool winds, and having briefly disposed of last night's homework problems plunge at once into urgent talk about who was friends with whom, who had fallen out, who was jealous. Later in the day, at break and lunch time, similar groups could be found beside the playing fields, in the wood, even on cold days in the coke-fumed boiler house. After the school day, a leisurely walk home might provide even more scope for woman-talk.

'Truth, dare, promise, love or kiss.'

That was a favourite girls' game. If you chose 'dare' your playmates might offer a physical challenge such as wall climbing. 'Promise' would perhaps require a pledge of future naughtiness, risking the wrath of authority; the demand might be to ask some outrageous question in a stern teacher's lesson. More often, however, as we grew towards the teen years, we would opt for truth or love. 'Kiss' was a requirement to kiss someone and seldom chosen, but 'truth' and 'love' challenged the victim to disclose truthfully her emotional state. 'Who do you love?' or 'Is it true that you've fallen out with X?' would follow the choice, at once plunging the fascinated playmates into intimate heart-to-heart confidences.

The loves, in our all-female culture, were on the whole single-sex affairs, though never to my knowledge physically expressed apart from walking with arms around each other's waists. In the Lower School years we were acting out the intricate couplings and webs of intrigue for which Angela Brazil had prepared us. 'Best friends' were quarrelled with, exchanged, whispered about. Torrid notes were written, plots hatched. Tears and emotional reconciliations added to the drama. Then there were 'pashes', passions for older girls or for teachers. So fashionable was this condition that it was virtually obligatory for eleven, twelve, thirteen year olds to choose an object of adoration, first simulate and then persuade

86

themselves into an obsessive emotion. In these states we were content to worship from afar. As a verse-maker I was in demand, for I would supply customised sentimental ditties in praise of the idol. Sexually most of us were ignorant and immature, though among over-fourteens some few had boyfriends. Even then, to be sure, 'going out with' meant literally that. In those days, at least in the circles I moved in, 'nice girls don't' was the accepted wisdom.

I knew no boys. Sometimes I sighed for the social kudos of boasting a boyfriend, but in fact felt no natural urge for the company of the abhorred male. Accordingly my first real falling in love was with a girl some two years my senior, met not at school but at church. Enid was a dark-haired, dark-eyed dynamo of energy, enthusiasm and earnestness, a singer with a contralto voice to which I, unmusical I, listened with rapture. I was not the only one who found her attractive. At seventeen Enid was already engaged to be married. Her mother kept a guest house. Airmen had been billeted with them, and Charlie had captivated the schoolgirl Enid before the end of war and his demobilisation sent him home to Sussex. Enid therefore, securely and chastely awaiting her future wedding and marking time as a junior civil servant, had time to devote to me. We became close friends. To me at that time homosexuality was as yet unheard of, undreamt of, let alone the lovely physicality of lesbian embraces. What on earth can I have hoped for? When, unable to resist the urge, I declared my love, Enid reacted with comforting but distancing words.

'I believe I've read somewhere about that kind of friendship,' she told me, carefully sympathetic but dry-eyed as she confronted my sobbing. 'It's not supposed to be healthy. We'd better pray about it.' Enid had acquired from her Charlie a simplified fundamentalist Christianity which had the answer to everything. This she pressed upon me. By the time we had this conversation I was already in its grip. Its grip, or hers?

# THE NEW MATHEMATICS

One and one and one make three
and two and two make four;
so numeracy starts, but life
has other sums in store.

One and one and one make One:
the trinitarians said it,
To theological niceties
we give but little credit,

but lovers claim that one and one
make one for evermore,
so two and two, we must conclude,
make two instead of four.

But what if there's an overlap
and two and two are three?
Whether to add or to divide
is love's perplexity.

Let x and y be bracketed
and y and z a pair,
and x and z of one accord,
contented with their share –

then one and one and one make one
in circularity,
and love's largesse to each and all
is multiplied by three.

\* \* \* \* \* \*

## ADVANCED NEW MATHEMATICS

And now suppose another 'set'
connecting v with z.
Of this fourth factor in the sum
what can be wisely said?

If y allows a line drawn in
connecting her with v
two intersecting triangles
make good geometry.

Come threefold love and fourfold love
and hundredfold the fruit!
All forms of love are forms of God,
the ultimate pursuit.

# 13. The ultimate pursuit

All forms of love are forms of God,
the ultimate pursuit.

Fifteen year old Anne would I think have recognised that statement. Certainly she was unable to disentangle human love from love of God. Nor can I, now. But whereas then it was a matter of practical concern and acute anxiety, now I can relax. If as Quakers say – echoing profounder wisdoms – there is 'that of God' in everyone, we are perhaps only playing with words here.

For most of my life I would have described myself as a lover of God. This has been the hub, the hinge, the axis, the still point; that which unified all my warring elements. I seldom use the word 'God' now. It is too heavy, loaded with worn-out icons, dragging connotations of a Great Supernatural Person. What then does it mean, to be a God-lover? I am still working that out, and will be, no doubt, as long as I live. 'All forms of love are forms of God.' There are the human loves, so many kinds, including altruism. Then there are other loves: love of the world, of beauty, of the arts, of thought. There is the sheer amazing givenness of life, a welling up of response to some energy greater than oneself. There is the corporate aspect of religious life, in which the collective psyche of the group, both conscious and unconscious, allows individuals to transcend themselves. All these are parts of it, aspects of God-loving.

There are places, those with a feel for such things assert, that are 'thin'. At holy sites like Delphi or Iona the veil between visible and invisible is so thin that you can feel divinity seeping through. I don't know. I have a religious temperament, but not that sort of equipment. Yet I do know that there are *times*, staging posts in our lives, when we ourselves are 'thin'. One such time, already described, occurred when I was nine and ten, coinciding with the awakening to self-reflexive consciousness. Another was at fifteen and sixteen, this time bound up with the awakenings of adolescence.

In mid-teens the psyche is at its most sensitive. For some it is a time of life as prone to crass religious enthusiasms and conversions as to erotic muddle. Youngsters today are better informed about sex, though not noticeably less muddled. They are less informed about God, though not less misled. At fifteen, sixteen, I was outwardly a cheerful intelligent girl, somewhat cast down about leaving school but well adjusted and taking life in her stride. Inwardly I was also a quivering jelly, skinless, boneless and shapeless.

It does not surprise me that my 'vision' recurred at this time, never afterwards to return. Though I had abandoned the Methodist Sunday school, church parade with the Guides had quickened my interest in the Baptist church to which the Guide company was attached. The preacher was eloquent, and I could enjoy a good sermon. Watching a baptismal service in which adults underwent total immersion, I was profoundly stirred.

And then there was Enid. The church was not, for a Baptist foundation, especially evangelical, but Enid was. Her fiancé came of a fiercely fundamentalist family, and Enid had bought the whole package. Zealously she proselytised me, and I was ready enough to be swept off my feet both by my friend and her God. Together we lived on the crest of a frothing wave, surfing rather than diving. I am tempted to describe it as a heady experience, but the head was scarcely involved. Better metaphors might be the heart racing, lungs gasping, arms flung aloft.

However, I never entirely abandon my head! Even with Enid I would dispute when my head raised objections. She plied me with books from evangelical presses, but I craved stronger meat. From the library I borrowed theological works, reading at random whatever came to hand. This, incidentally, precipitated an unexpected lurch along the

91

feminist path.

I had been reading Emil Brunner, and innocently went to ask my minister a question arising from the book. His response shocked me.

'Good gracious, what's a pretty little girl doing worrying her head over books like that?'

I never forgave him. But he did me good; he stiffened the flabby feminist sinews. That same year, I received similar treatment from my dentist. In his waiting-room I had been reading Virgil's *Eclogues* in the Penguin translation. As I laid it down in the surgery the dentist raised his eyebrows and made some remark akin to the minister's. I was humiliated, enraged, at once an enlisted feminist.

Feminism lasted. Evangelicalism didn't, though for years I stayed with church, for where else was there to go, pursuing the Grail? I had to, I still have to, explore that ineffable reality than which nothing is more precious.

Ineffable: that which cannot be put into words. It was words I needed, I see that now. The magic at the bottom of the garden, the 'lyric thrill', the nameless pull of the numinous – for these I wanted a language, and Christianity seemed to provide one. Later, as I grew up, I rejected doctrine after doctrine, and drifted into an agnostic wilderness, disappointed. Later still, in the 1960s, John Robinson's *Honest to God* offered a glimpse of how after all Christianity, differently interpreted, might provide the language I so needed. Somehow I made my way back into a church, studied theology systematically, reinterpreted the faith for others . . . then after twenty years became too heretical to remain. But all that is another story.

## The ultimate pursuit

I have sought sorrowing
Mourning your death.
I have sought singing,
breathing your breath.

Absence inscrutable,
gouged from my knowing;
presence immutable,
root of my growing –

you are the magnet
that pulls from within,
you are the dragnet
fishing me in.

Force of velocity,
stillness of stone,
love's reciprocity
felt when alone –

how can I know you
or know you a lie?
Nothing can show you
and nothing deny.

Images founder,
words lose their role,
yet in profounder
silence of soul,

past each illusion,
searching and losing,
through all confusion
you are my choosing.

It was at that Baptist church that I met the Indians. During the war this congregation had instituted a 'social hour' after Sunday evening service, for the benefit of service men and women stationed in Blackpool, and this became a regular feature of the church programme even after the war. Each week a volunteer would be master of ceremonies and had the task of arranging a concert party. Sometimes Enid would sing, I would recite.

The two Indian men were not servicemen, but civil servants in the India Department which had been evacuated to Blackpool. Both were educated men with British MA degrees, one from an Indian Christian background and the other a convert from Hinduism. They would be surprised to know how deeply they influenced me. When Mr Koshi was to take the chair at the next social hour, he asked me to learn and recite two poems of Rabindranath Tagore. The book he lent me was *Gitanjali* (Song Offerings).

I read, I re-read, I was transported. W.B. Yeats, in his introduction to the book, had written
I have carried the manuscript of these translations about with me for days, reading it in railway trains, or on the tops of omnibuses and in restaurants, and I have often had to close it lest some stranger would see how much it moved me.

Mr Koshi and his friend opened India for me. And they gave me a new perspective on Christianity.

'You know the trouble with Christianity? It's so humiliating.'

I was startled. They explained. Those doctrines of sin and redemption, of helpless need of a saviour, were demeaning of human dignity. I began to read the Upanishads, those ancient insights of India. The spiritual quest, it seemed, was not to abase oneself but to discover one's true and best essence in the One divine Self. *Tat tvam asi*: thou art That. So simple, so difficult. So many questions raised.

Steps heard in the playroom, said Tagore,
echo from star to star.
He who treads is weaving webs of *maya*,
allowing us to play
in this his playhouse of unnumbered forms
till we discern the formless.

The angel of annunciations
put on a brown face:
small brown man, family in Bengal,
cultivated accent, MA Oxon,
offering his cherished poet.

Tagore uncurtained India
as Guerber Greece.
Light, eye kissing light, heart sweetening light!
– he sang, as travellers do who celebrate
sun on the Parthenon.

Light! limpid Mediterranean air,
pellucid, crystal, Apollonian.
Light! Christ on a Levantine hill:
transfigured incandescence.
Light! the Gita's terrible theophany,
God effulgent shown to Arjuna.

It does not yet appear what we shall be,
but when we see him we shall be like him,
the apostle John and Prajapati claim.
Transfigured, or extinguished?
Are we not like those little Indian lights,
the flickering leaf-boat lights
pushed out on holy Ganges from the ghats

to gutter and drown: Indian oil of spikenard,
folly, no doubt, to the Greeks?

In deep darkness fall
the followers of action,
into deeper darkness
seekers after knowledge.
Thus the Upanishad.

Yet in the hidden catacomb of self
that Self may bloom.
The announcing angel does not ask for lamps.


\* \* \* \* \* \* \*


Where shall we find that One? – the students asked.
Prajapati looked at them; replied,
Adorn yourselves and dress in splendid clothes.
Gaze in a bowl of water. What is there?
We see ourselves there, Master Prajapati,
but we are robed in splendour.
Even so is Brahman, brahmacarins. Go,
says Prajapati, with your hearts in peace.

Bring me, Svetaketu, fruit of the banyan tree.
Break it. What do you see?
　　Tiny seeds, my father.
Break one. What do you see?
　　Nothing at all, my father.
From that unseeable essence comes the tree.
That, my son, is Brahman, that is Atman.
Svetaketu, Thou Art That.

Where is the salt, my son, you put in the cup of water?
    Father, I cannot see.
Taste the water this side.
    Father, it is salt.
Taste the water that side.
    Father, it is salt.
Even so is Truth, that Self, my Svetaketu.
That is Atman. Thou Art That.

# 14. Work

No knight in shining armour rescued me. Dry-eyed, stiff upper-lipped, sixteen next week, I quitted school. So acute was the pain that I severed all connection with school, never revisited it. I ceased to see my schoolfriends, all of whom were going on to sixth form and university.

Higher education being denied, I was determined at least to be among books. Almost at once, I began work as a junior assistant in the public library. In half a century's retrospect, it seems to me that I was busy, buoyant, inquisitive, far from despondent. For the first fortnight, admittedly, I dropped into bed every night at an early hour, exhausted by unaccustomed physical labour. The lifting and carrying performed by library assistants, and indeed by librarians at all levels below the managerial, is seldom suspected by the public. There is the constant shelving of returned books, the daily rearranging and dusting, the occasional major removals of stock from place to place, the sorting of discarded material or – in those days – books to be rebound, the crating of consignments for other libraries, the unpacking of supplies from booksellers: donkey work. But all the time it was books we were handling, books which we could dip into, learn about, learn from. They fitted into classification schemes of immense interest and complexity, schemes that provided a young assistant with an invaluable overview of the whole of knowledge. Avenues of wonder were revealed, glimpses of art and science, thought and imagination. To me, it was all delight; and remained so.

'Such a nice clean job, too,' people would remark patronisingly, unaware of the dust solidifying under every assistant's fingernails. Library stocks were older and dustier in those days than they are now. The grimiest task I ever had the misfortune to undertake came a few years later. Most of the schools in the town held collections of books on loan from the public library. One year, the town council in its collective unwisdom decreed that this service should no longer be supported. All the books were accordingly called in, many thousands of them. The library could neither accommodate them nor jettison them. Space was found in the dreadful infernal regions, a murky sulphurous cellar where the coke boilers were stoked. Here the books were piled in an enormous heap some four feet high and extending over an area the size of a modest bedroom. Twelve months later the town council, revising its collective wisdom, decided after all to reinstate the service. At this juncture it fell to me to rescue what volumes had survived the year's fumes, coke dust and merciless heaping. I spent every morning for six weeks, filthy and coughing, below stairs on this sorting exercise. Every meal I ate tasted of coke. But by the time I emerged I knew a lot about children's books.

For the first year, however, the work was menial but carefully varied. The day was divided into 90 minute periods, at the end of which all duties changed – perhaps from shelving to issuing books, from packing or unpacking to filing cards or affixing labels. On my first day, I had been told that I would finish at 6.00 p.m. It happened that at five I had been placed out of sight in a corner of the reference library, where I was humbly sticking labels into new books. The clock crept slowly, oh unbearably slowly, towards six. The librarian on duty gave no sign. I worked on. Quarter past, half past, going on to seven. Dare I speak? Dare I desert my task? At last, as seven o'clock closing time approached, the librarian rose and noticed me.

'You still here? What time are you supposed to finish?'
Me, shyly: 'Er . . . six o'clock, actually.'
'Good heavens, run along, child. And remember, you don't have to be told to go home. This isn't school, you know.'

I knew. Never had I finished a school day so late, aching, hungry. Yet I was eager for the next day.

For three months I worked in the lending department, followed by three months each in reference, cataloguing and acquisitions. This was the junior year, in which we were familiarised with at least the humbler levels of each aspect of the work. At the same time our professional education began, at a night school class taught by the senior librarians. Here we prepared for the Library Association's entrance exam, studying library organisation, classification, cataloguing, book production (papermaking, printing, illustration processes, binding), bibliography, reference materials and twentieth century English literature. None of us, teachers or learners, could then have conceived of the coming world of information technology. Computers? – we didn't even use typewriters.

Almost everything was in longhand. Two typewriters had indeed recently been acquired for the cataloguing department, where professional staff were engaged on the years-long task of recataloguing the entire chain of nine libraries, but this was not work for juniors. One day in my first week in the cataloguing room, I was at the junior's desk, painstakingly entering details of new books into a large ledger called an accessions register. The chief librarian entered. It was my first glimpse of this awesome figure, at least since the brief interview at which I had been offered the job. He paused at my desk and surveyed the ruled page.

'THAT,' thundered the chief, 'is not library handwriting!' I shook in my shoes as he sternly ordered me to amend my handwriting immediately if I wished to survive my six-month period of temporary trial employment.

Recently, when as a user of that same library I was filling in a request form, the librarian complimented me on my neat writing. Laughing, I told him why it was acquired, but the librarian was too bewildered to be amused. He could just about conceive of a library without computers, but without *typewriters* . . . ?

We worked a forty-hour week, soon reduced to thirty-eight hours, and pay began at thirty shillings a week. We were in fact paid monthly, and in cash. Each pay day a man from the town hall arrived with a heavy bag, and a senior librarian sat by him as we queued eagerly to sign for our coins and notes. Much of mine went to my mother for food, but I was allowed to keep the rest and encouraged to learn how to budget for clothes, toiletries, toothpaste, towels, bus fares, church collections, cinema tickets, stationery. For the first two years mother undertook to buy the really expensive items such as shoes and coats. She probably, though I cannot recall this, helped me towards my first holiday.

Part of the training of junior assistants was their deployment at branch libraries. We would be instructed to go as relief staff for a morning or afternoon or a whole week, either to help at a busy branch or to take over the desk at a small one-horse establishment. This we enjoyed – the change of scene, the time spent travelling (strictly monitored lest we should be tempted to shopping or idling), the freedom from senior supervision. During my junior year I served in five different outlying libraries, so what happened next seemed to follow naturally. Yet looking back now, I am astonished. In my thirteenth month, aged barely seventeen, I was placed in charge of a branch library. How could They, the Powers-that-were, have entrusted such responsibility to a schoolgirl?

Hawes Side was a small branch, needing only two assistants to cover, between them, its limited opening hours, and together to cope with its few busy periods. Margaret, who was junior even to me, took turns with me to staff the branch during its quiet mornings, the other one reporting to the central library. This kept us in touch with other units of the system, continued our in-house training, and allowed us the pleasure of socialising with a larger staff.

I was in clover. A library all of my own, with freedom to arrange my work, help readers, devise displays, request books! Already I felt like a librarian. Better still, there were long hours with little custom, when having completed the chores I could read undisturbed. Much of the reading was study, to be sure, for the first seven years of my working life were spent laboriously gaining my ALA (Associate of the Library Association). Most people acquired this in two years at college, but this was not possible for me. The local authority would make no grant, and in any case I had to be earning. After that first year of elementary evening classes I ploughed a rather lonely furrow, working through correspondence courses. At the same time, however, undeservedly blessed with so much unsupervised free time at work, I was reading widely, educating myself, trying to be my own sixth form and university. Lacking direction, my reading was haphazard, unstructured, uncritical. Butterfly fashion, I flitted from art history to biography, poetry to philosophy, psychology to literary theory. There must have been much I failed to understand, much for which I had no context, no pegs or pigeonholes for what I discovered.

But the excitement of serendipity, those magnificent expanding horizons of thought! Each book left me hungry for a dozen more.

There is a sort of greed about reading. For librarians, who handle books not in scores but in thousands, there grows an insatiable appetite which must always be tinged with despair. Never in a lifetime or a hundred lifetimes could one read all those desirable volumes, and all the time fresh books pour from the presses. Shall I ever reach an old age serene enough to be content with the books I own?

This absurdly easy lifestyle at Hawes Side branch lasted for four and a half years, the years of growing up. It probably spoiled me for ever for really hard work of any kind. Having to organise both my work and my studies, and do both for the most part alone, certainly equipped me for many later situations. But it also left me uneasy in team work, rebellious about taking orders, used to getting my own way and devising my own systems. That is a self-portrait all too recognisable still. How do my friends put up with me?

The hours at work – I cannot truthfully call them working hours – were long. Once or twice a week 'split days' with three hours off in the afternoon meant that a six-hour day would not finish until 7.00 p.m. Add study time at home, and playtime is limited. Was Jill a dull girl? I was sheltered, innocent, studious. Most of my partying was at church socials, the church badminton club, the library staff association, an amateur drama group. At seventeen I had never touched alcohol, never heard of drugs, never been to a dance and never been kissed.

But when you are seventeen anything, everything seems possible. The lifetime ahead is forever, for growing old is unimaginable. And meanwhile the sap rises, it is spring, you blush, you tingle, you run. I ran everywhere, as unable as I had been at four years old to restrict my steps to adult walking pace. One day, running as usual along a street, I halted by a patch of waste ground. It had long grass, full grown featherlight seeded grassheads, swayed by a Blackpool breeze. I remembered my vow at the age of nine, knowing with a thrill of triumph that I had not forgotten how it felt. How could I? I was going to be a poet.

Or was I? A self-conscious teenager, I had ceased to show my mother what I wrote. I knew no-one else who admitted to reading poetry, let alone sympathised with the odd affectation of writing it. Poetry, I concluded, was generally regarded as a private vice, an occasion for shame. But I could be a librarian. I enjoyed the work, scored high marks in each year's exams, and at Hawes Side had premature responsibility with opportunities for initiative. Very well then: I would rise to the top of the profession, be among the few eminent women there!

Except for Saturdays, there was only one busy time of day at Hawes Side. Until four o'clock we had a mere trickle of fiction readers and market gardeners seeking horticultural books, for this was still a semi-rural area on the edge of town, known as The Moss. Many families were interrelated. The register of readers was heavily weighted with Carrs and Cardwells. It was wise never to speak disrespectfully of residents, for they were sure to be second cousins of the person you were talking to. However, the library was situated between a primary school and a secondary school, so the children's section was well used after four o'clock. I allowed selected reliable children behind the desk to stamp issued books, a privilege much sought after. So when a memo from the chief librarian was dispatched to all branches, urging branch librarians to liaise with schools, I was all enthusiasm.

I was twenty. With superb confidence that I could beat the teachers at their own trade on their own ground, I sailed into both schools and breezily asked the head teachers for permission to talk to their pupils. Doubtless taken aback, they both agreed. In the primary school I went from classroom to classroom, passed round book jackets and picture books, distributed library membership cards. The following day at four o'clock a noisy swarm of children came waving their blue cards, jostling for admission. It was therefore with redoubled confidence that I kept my appointment at the secondary school a few days later. – and was not a little disconcerted to find that the headmistress had quite forgotten our arrangement.

'Well, you can't go round the classes, that's out of the question. But since you're here, you may as well address assembly.'

It was 9.00 a.m., there was no time to think. She swept me into the hall and up on to the stage. My classroom technique was no use here, my visual aids useless. Well that my mother had taught me never to fear platforms or public speaking! I delivered some sort of impromptu talk and left membership cards for distribution. I cannot have done it well, but at least I must have done it effectively, for the result was as striking as before. From that week, junior borrowing figures at the little library soared. Even the Powers-that-were noticed. And so my ambition crystallized, modified: I would specialise, I would become a children's librarian.

## 15. Growing up

War was behind us. A new Britain was under construction. There was relief, optimism, gaiety in spite of the problems. Rationing continued. When I started work in 1947 the central library had a small canteen concession; not that we had a canteen, but some of us ate lunch on the premises, so the points system allowed us to make small purchases. I only recall this because having used canteen points one day to buy corned beef for sandwiches, we discovered there was no margarine for the bread. The staffroom cupboard was empty except for a jar of strawberry jam, so with this we moistened the bread, pressing our corned beef between the sticky slices. I cannot recommend this recipe!

We girls felt the new age had dawned when Dior's New Look held the headlines. Instead of skimpily cut skirts and dresses with the wartime 'Utility' label, Dior suddenly decreed calf-length skirts with ample material. I strutted into the staffroom in a dazzling buttercup yellow New Look dress adorned with big black polka dots: a sensation! I still mourn for the glorious skirts of the 1950s – gathered, flared, pleated, half-circle or even full-circle, sometimes layered or frilled, sometimes worn over stiff layered petticoats. Where can be the joy of twirling and pirouetting, for girls in sober leggings or jeans or minis?

By contrast, information hitherto secret was beginning to be released, so that people could at last glimpse the scale of devastation and suffering the war had imposed. The greatest shock came with the revelations from the Nazi camps. Entering central library one day, I came upon a group of horrified staff gathered around a new book. The discussion, it appeared, was over whether this volume could be allowed on to the open public shelves. When I was able to make my way through to reach the book, I realised why. Here were photographs taken when a camp (was it Auschwitz?) and its ghastly half-dead inhabitants were discovered.

Since then, television has familiarised us with too many horrors. We have seen Ethiopia, Bhopal, Vietnam, Bosnia . . . more. Sensibilities are blunted. We have gazed on serpent-haired Medusa and our hearts are turned to stone. As a generation we have taken refuge in cynicism, a defence against feeling. But it was not so then, and those indistinct black and white photographs brought shock, disbelief, grief.

As yet I knew little about the previous war. Having read Rupert Brooke but not yet Wilfred Owen, I had given the first world war little thought. Then one sleepy afternoon at Hawes Side, when I was alone in the library, a lame man with a walking stick entered. We fell into conversation, perhaps about the book he was returning. Somehow he began to speak of his experiences in the terrible trenches of 1914-18, saying that for years he had been unable to do so. Now he realised that there was a new generation – I was one – to whom it was either forgotten history or completely unknown. He felt, like the Ancient Mariner, compelled to tell his tale. I listened spellbound, appalled. Never had I heard a firsthand account of such suffering, such evil, such waste. Surely there must be other ways of settling disputes, better ways of being human? Yet even now it seems that the whole shameful history of the century has failed to teach us.

But I was young and the world was beautiful. Life had present fun and future promise; and I had friends. From earliest schooldays friendship has been of supreme importance to me. Having virtually nothing in the way of family life meant that I grew up without family feeling. Though I have a son whom I love deeply and admire intensely, I have not been a good mother. This is cause for shame but perhaps not for surprise. However, I am willing to claim a modest expertise in friendship.

> In the art of friendship
> we hesitantly build
> degrees of skill.
> Each fresh assay begins an unmapped sortie.
> Let us prospect for oil.

A formulation of dissident elements,
interplay of light from prismatic surfaces,
collocation of ideas . . .
call it communication;
but communication began, and subterraneously
continues on a less articulate plane,
the level of shrugged shoulder, raised eyebrow,
where lips, fingers, posture make their tentative statements.

In the integration of *I* and *Thou*
there is no precise juxtaposition
but folded strata
and innumerable loose ends.
Here we unwind simplicity
out of a psychic labyrinth,
affinity not deserved nor understood,
only received as grace.

Enid duly married her Charlie and went to live in Sussex. A few months later I spent a week with them, observed their newlywed happiness, and came to terms with the fact that I had no further claim on Enid. Just as well, for they had decided to offer themselves for missionary work. The following year the couple enrolled at a Bible college where their fundamentalist Christianity was reinforced and where they acquired enough Portuguese to work in a Portuguese territory. In 1950 they set off to save the souls of the benighted heathen in Nyasaland. I sometimes wonder what became of them, whether they did less harm than good, and whether they later modified their views.

Getting over Enid, I was content with ordinary friendships. Though well aware of the strong social pressures to acquire a boyfriend and then a wedding ring, I could raise no enthusiasm either for the idea of marriage or for any young man of my acquaintance. Nor, apparently, did any of them look in my direction. In any case, I saw myself as a career woman, and our local authority, which I took to be typical, did not employ married women. A wedding meant the sack, and I do not refer to bedlinen.

My closest friends at this time were Eileen and Beryl. With one or other I spent my Sundays (library assistants of course worked on Saturdays) and with each in turn I went on holiday.

It was with Beryl that I first discovered the Lake District. We stayed at a cheap guest house in a remote spot, with a mile to walk to a bus which could take us into Keswick, The farmhouse could accommodate eight guests, but had no bathroom and the privy was far away at the end of the farmyard. In case of urgent need during the night – when in the pitch dark no guest could have found that distant throne room – each bedroom had a zinc bucket. Beryl and I endured miseries rather than use ours. However, the food was wholesome and the proprietors kind.

We arrived on Saturday evening, in darkness. Sunday morning we set out for a walk, promising to be back for lunch. We had clear instructions about the route from our hosts, but no map. We walked. And walked. How was it nothing seemed to tally with what we had been told? We began to ask our way, but as we had only the name of the farmhouse and by now were far from it, little help was forthcoming. Alarmed though not panic-stricken, we were in fact more distressed by the hunger raised by fresh air and exercise. Pockets were ransacked. Not a penny piece between us; we had only gone out for an hour's stroll. Two toffees and one cigarette. I disliked smoke, but a few shared puffs were solace just then. How we found our way back I do not remember, but our kindly hosts were greatly concerned: two young girls, lost on their first day! Later in the week we got lost again, in bracken so tall we could see nothing. But it was all wonder. Two wide-eyed townees, we tramped and gazed, giggled and gloried. Fells, ghylls, lakes, rocks, all lovelier than I could have dreamt. My son was taken to Lakeland from a few weeks old, and throughout his childhood. That seemed good and right. Yet for Beryl and me there was a fine piquancy, an extra intensity, in the response of an adolescent, perhaps at the optimum age for feeling, who had never seen such countryside before. Years later, a middle aged woman talking with an impetuous young man, it was Lakeland imagery that came to mind.

## WATER SKIER

'We run to extremes,' he said,
'we adolescents. Someone should teach us patience.'
(Adolescents? They still use that word?
How quaint they are, the young.)

Spurt of the speedboat tensed
the skier's line. Out on a flung arc,
crossing his wake, he failed
to straighten – plunged.

'There's countryside ahead,' I tried to tell him,
'for middle aged restraint.'
(Now take your wet suit off, I tell myself,
try on a tweed skirt.)

The holiday with Eileen was more urban. We stayed in York, in a private house. Our hosts were, I think, friends of friends of friends. Margaret and Laurence were a childless couple thrilled to have two surrogate daughters for a week. They protected us, they treated us to outings, they fed us till we staggered, and all for twenty-five shillings. (It was 1949.) They took us to *The Gondoliers*, my first ever Gilbert and Sullivan. So green was I that I sat mystified through the overture, wondering why the stage curtains had not opened; were they stuck? They took us to the racecourse, an equally dizzying experience. The horses plunged towards us, were gone in a second. What was there to see? Only the betting. Betweenwhiles, Eileen and I wandered about York, fascinated by the museums and buildings. Eileen haunted the antique shops, I the bookshops. We rowed on the Ouse, or more correctly Eileen rowed. Never muscular, I had not the strength to handle a heavy river rowboat, and as we had drifted carelessly downstream it took all Eileen's strength and stamina to get us back again. Without rancour, she blamed me for her blistered hands. All week we laughed, laughed at ourselves, at our foolishness and ignorance, at the care we took to split every item of expenditure exactly; laughed at the world, laughed, simply, with delight at being young, alive, full of hope.

Eileen and I had almost nothing in common, yet we were easy together and intimate. One Sunday we returned from some outing and called at my home before going to Eileen's for tea.

'Is someone with you?' called my mother from another room.
'No, only Eileen,' I replied thoughtlessly, to be hotly reprimanded by that young lady. When we reached her home, it was only justice that her mother happened to call from the kitchen,
'Have you brought someone in for tea?'
'No, only Anne,' was the inevitable response. There is much to be said for reaching a level of friendship in which each can take the other comfortably for granted.

Eileen was flirtatious, attractive and indeed had real beauty. She had a succession of boyfriends, and our elders muttered darkly. 'That one'll come to no good. She'll get herself in trouble.' She didn't. Like Enid, she married young.

I had friends, but then as now I loved sometimes to be solitary. Days off during the week, in lieu of Saturdays, and the afternoons of my 'split days' offered opportunity. In fine weather I would take my studies, or writing, or a book to read, and somewhere in busy Blackpool find a quiet place. There as often as not instead of opening my books I would sit in contemplation, thinking those 'thoughts of youth [which] are long, long thoughts', according to Longfellow. Such times are precious. Now, as a Quaker, I have belatedly discovered that they can also be shared.

For reasons I had not then articulated, I was drawn to rocks. On Blackpool's South Promenade there are ersatz artificial 'rocks', an attempt to add contour to an otherwise dull flat seafront. Even those would do; I was less critical then. The cliffs at the north end are almost as contrived, their 'rocks' equally phoney constructions, but of this I was probably unaware. It was a place for gazing out over the water, absorbing its ever changing colours and movement, a place to watch a sunset through to its dramatic end. (For some, the sun may sink behind hills or over plains. To one from a western coast, such sunsets are against nature: all proper suns go down into the sea.) There were a few rocks of a sort by the park lake too. Later I encountered real rocks, ancient rocks. Their magic is potent. I was over fifty before I analysed it, though analysis is too cerebral a term for the understanding that comes through contact with primordial earth.

# *AMONG ROCKS*

If rock moves, it is not in our time
    yet rock exerts a pressure.
Rock cannot insist. Its igneous whispers
    are courteous cajolers
assigning our appropriate response.
    Climb. Lean. Hold. Sit.

Rigid imperatives, yet flexible
    to hand and knee
    weather or temperament.

An urge to immobility among rocks
    is my persuader:
to lean, adjust one's weight to rock,
    ordering limbs,
breath, eyelids into impassivity,
    mimetic substance –
yet why seek the dead among the living?
    Some things move here.

That tree even in its austerity
    sends down pipettes,
sucks with the anxious vehemence of March,
    unclenches nerve tips –
slow motion work, as our perception measures
but in a palaeolithic calibration
    sizzles and flashes.

If rock moves, it is not in our time.
    Trees change faster
but still (even still) we cannot watch.
    Human, we've no fast winder.

Rampart of rock behind
    accepts tree teasing.
Flutter of shadows over its lit face
    does not disturb:
an hour's superficial patterning.

Should we not like the tree
    stand, stretch our fingers?

*Growing up*

This yoga of non-action may determine
    death by stagnation.

    Quick, mark the kestrel!
It soars on sunlight, stoops –
    treads air, suspended.
Yet it's the hovering compels attention:
    trying to be rock in air.
    You too, quickwing?

This hunger to be earth material
    as sure we shall be:
not a mere lust for permanence,
    still less the death wish
but clenching down into a depth of spirit
    so still it has no surface
where thought becomes impacted into rock.

    To be in these minutes rock.


\* \* \* \* \* \* \*


'You are the music while the music lasts.'


\* \* \* \* \* \* \*


We cannot synchronise incongruous clocks.
    Stone. Tree. Breath. Music.
Shorter than trees, longer than music, we
    after the last slow note

jerk, stretch, itch, tingle
    into activity.
The brain sets up its loom, opens for business.
    So much for music.

But rock – by this we are outstared.
    Rock – against which
our momentary splash of song becomes
    a note unnoticed –
how to be rock while rock lasts?
    Are we charged to learn
how to be schist or quartz?

The secret could be quite the opposite.
    Stone strives to be us.
You are the music while the human lasts.
    Earth comes to consciousness
when sundry sandgrains know they chafe themselves.

Rock being given, we readjust a kinship
    as we interiorise,
swallow these rocks even as they subsume us,
    trade flesh for flesh with grit.

# 16. Crowded rooms and mismatches

Besides bank holidays, assistants were allowed two weeks holiday per year. When possible I took one of my weeks at the time of the local drama festival. All aspiring amateur groups entered this event, and I would attend avidly every night. The group I belonged to was ambitiously named The Questors, after a well known London group, The Questors of Ealing, who had their own 'little theatre'. We, however, had only the large front room of our director's house for rehearsal space, and very crowded it became, what with actors and non-actors, props and improvised stage-sets, not to mention jealousies and outbursts of dramatic temperament.

The Questors seldom aspired beyond playing to charity groups. Mostly we performed comedy. The part I most enjoyed was that of a lovelorn secretary in a one-act farce. I was required to weep throughout the play, repeating the line 'Oh, Mr Aspinall!' in as many different ways as I could invent. However, once we staged a serious historical drama in which (my one and only leading part) I played Elizabeth Fry. I took this role with extreme and unnecessarily pious seriousness, even contriving a period of quiet meditation before each performance, to 'think myself into the part'. Was a breeze from the far distant future whispering that I would become a Quaker? A fanciful conceit; yet playing that part did indeed influence me.

But to return to holidays. Once a year I contrived to go away, even if it was only to Library Association summer school. My father was always agog on these occasions. Though he seldom at that time travelled himself, my father was a devotee of that railwayman's scripture, *Bradshaw's Railway Guide*. This immense compendium listed all timetables for British trains, and that at a period when every village had its station. How James Henry became so conversant with this great work I never understood. His brain must have contained something like a computer memory of timetables. Let someone mention a place, even without a suggestion of going there, and James Henry would at once reel off a series of train times with changes and connections. He was also not so much punctual as absurdly early for everything, so whenever I went away he would insist on carrying my bags to the station and have me there long before the train was due. To be fair to my father, he truly cherished his daughter. It was I who could not reciprocate. My life has held other such mismatches. Perhaps I deserved them.

Once long ago he had been a daily commuter; indeed my parents had met on a train. Now he seldom left home except for walks. But in 1949, the year I was eighteen and my mother fifty, my parents took a holiday. This was cause for astonishment, even though finances were easier now that I was working and mother had more pupils. And indeed the holiday was only a week in Bridlington. Still, it was a surprise. What was going on? It was seven years before I discovered the answer.

And after all I did not ponder long over the question. A self-centred teenager, I paid scant attention to my parents' affairs except in so far as they concerned me. The interest of their holiday for me was that I was left to fend for myself. Mother left me thirty shillings, far more than I would need, she assured me, for a week's food. This was the year of my York holiday with a week's full board for twenty five shillings. Needless to say, I spent the thirty shillings prodigally and lived hungrily for the last two days. For their homecoming tea, I recall with embarrassment, all I managed to provide was one fish cake apiece, a pitiful lone offering each on its ungarnished plate. My parents were forbearing enough not to complain.

The joy of their week for me was the sense that home – that is to say, that part of the house which we rented – was all mine. No sooner had my elders departed than I looked critically around the living room, crowded with their belongings. All the pictures and ornaments ('clutter', I called them) I swept into hiding. From the library I brought a row of poetry books which I arranged on the now pleasingly bare sideboard. There ! that looked like *my* room, I thought, exulting. I can even remember the books. I was reading the Romantics and the Victorians at the time, so the sideboard supported Keats and Shelley, Tennyson and Browning – and the beguiling Swinburne under whose spell I had briefly fallen, not for the sense but the sound.

This playing at independence for a week was connected with a restless awareness that all my former school friends were departing to university. I alone, it seemed, was condemned to stay at home. Was there no way out? I would not be a qualified librarian for years yet. There was no hope of moving from Blackpool until then. For weeks I racked my brains. I scanned the columns of the local paper for cheap lodgings, and even went secretly to look at two. But the arithmetic defeated me. My meagre salary simply would not pay for a bedsit, taking into account living expenses and the cost of my study courses and exam fees. I am glad, now, that my parents knew nothing of this. They would have been hurt that I was so anxious to escape.

Escape what? My unsatisfactory home, the shame and irritation of my father's inadequacies. The frustration of being stranded at home when my contemporaries from school had flown the nest. The vulgarity of Blackpool, the provincialism of small public libraries. As though the burden of librarianship studies were not enough, I took extra correspondence courses too, in the subjects that touched my heart: modern poetry, writing, religion. Inwardly, I was in retreat – beginning to be the girl who runs backwards, ill at ease even with those she likes, unable to communicate her quest for the Grail. Though not outwardly moody (my mother's lessons in self-control still bear fruit), I was in a well-hidden teenage ferment, a mixture of conflicting dreams, depressions and exaltations, arrogant superiority and timid insecurity. I found my colleagues pleasant company, but despised their lack of interest in anything intellectual or literary.

117

Then suddenly there was Michael.

I was nineteen. It was my morning at central library. I went as usual to the staffroom to hang my coat and mingle with the crowd before we all dispersed to departments. A new member of staff was sitting quietly in a corner, observing us with clear thoughtful steady eyes. He was briefly introduced, no more than a name. Some discussion was taking place, I no longer know what about. Michael listened, then made some calmly penetrating remark that drew my instant attention. This man was clearly different, a thinker, a reader.

'Across a crowded room,' as a popular song of the period had it, I was magnetised. I took in the slim figure, the shabby brown sports jacket, the pale delicate face, those perceptive eyes. Love at first sight? There can be no such thing, for love grows with acquaintance. There is, though, a mechanism of attraction which can and does operate in a flash. Unfortunately nature's chemistry is not necessarily a two-way affair. I felt it, he did not. Later in my life, two men felt it for me – in one case it was literally across a crowded room – yet all I could feel for them was pity. Mismatches.

By the time my morning stint was over Michael was already in the staffroom again, eating his lunch. Before I left for Hawes Side we had some brief conversation, no word of which can I remember. But I left the building telling myself firmly, jauntily, 'I shall marry that man or die in the attempt.' I died in the attempt.

It is a significant measure of adolescent self-absorption that I recall little between 1950 and 1955 except my personal preoccupations, chiefly my professional concerns and Michael; little of the world at large, little even of my parents. If now I catch myself judging a young man or young woman as inconsiderate, I remember wryly the absolute self-centredness of my own youth. Never call the young unfeeling. It is precisely because they are so busy feeling so intensely that they have no eyes for those around them.

In one astonishing morning, I had changed my mind about the marriage question. This had now to be reconciled with professional ambition, so I was quick to construct a new castle in the air. The revised scenario now appeared as follows. Michael was four years older than me but we were due to qualify about the same time. We would then apply for – and naturally obtain with ease – jobs in senior positions in the same authority, one which employed married women. I saw us returning at evening to the marital love-nest, eager to discuss our day's work, supporting each other towards further promotion. The question of children cannot, I think, have presented itself to me.

The subject and object of these dreams was of course quite unaware of them. Michael quickly made it clear – he probably had to, in a staffroom crowded with marriage-ripe girls – that he was a determined bachelor, single-mindedly concerned with becoming a chartered librarian as soon as possible. This I airily disregarded. I knew he had no girlfriend, and was certain beyond all doubt that he was my destiny. I can even remember some confident verses I wrote on the subject.

> Since you're professed a Benedick
> Then I'll be Beatrice
> And scorn you now
> With merry vow
> And feminine caprice.
>
> Go tread your unmolested path;
> I'll take the other way
> And gaily sing
> Of anything
> That makes a maiden's day,
> But not a word of love, my dear
> And not a word of you,

For youth's a gay
Glad holiday
And bachelors are few –

So few that it will not be long,
I fondly prophesy
Till you abjure
The false allure
Of self-sufficiency.
And then, my lordly Benedick,
Remember Beatrice,
Whose former scorn
Is all forsworn
To bow to your caprice.

So much for feminism! As I noted earlier, in the postwar years sexual mores reverted to something more old fashioned than the urgent couplings of wartime partners about to be separated. It was an unwritten law that girls took no initiatives beyond conveying a friendly interest. You had to wait for a boy to ask you out, usually to a dance or cinema or coffee bar, then allow him gently to push the business on. If then the boy was not content with slow progress you would be obliged, the agony aunts scolded us, to make sure he toed the line.

Accordingly I waited, steadfastly disregarding all others, in my own view a virtuous heroine in some romance of lifelong fidelity. There was of course nothing to prevent a young lady from putting herself where her intended victim would notice her. In this, fate appeared indeed to be obliging me. Michael was placed in charge of a branch library, one actually on the route I walked to Hawes Side. It was remarkable, and of course remarked by others, how much business suddenly necessitated visits to Highfield from the Hawes Side branch librarian. Keeping a close tally on Michael's duty hours, I could also just happen to be walking down Highfield Road when his bus arrived.

'I know how it feels
To have wings on your heels
And to fly down the street in a trance.
You fly down the street
On the chance that you'll meet,
And you meet, not really by chance'
as Anna sings in *The King and I*.

So we met frequently, though the meetings (when not 'by chance') still tended to be in crowded rooms. We were friends, we had topics worth talking about – books and ideas. But the word I waited for did not come.

# 17. Modes of learning

There was a stirring among the staff, a rumour discreetly circulating: the children's librarian was leaving to be married. I danced with impatience, bit my nails with doubt. Would They, could They, appoint someone still not qualified? I let it be known that I was eager for the post, hoping that my success with junior readers out in the sticks had been noted. Long weeks of uncertainty passed. Yes! the Powers-that-were would allow me the privilege of doing a chartered librarian's work for a clerical assistant's wage. So elated was I, it scarcely occurred to me that the authority was getting a bargain, but no trade unionist blew the whistle. I moved to central library and took charge of the children's library. This was to be the capital of my modest empire, from which I would make forays to visit schools around the town.

The departing librarian briefly briefed me. These were the needs, these the tasks, these her methods. Then, conspiratorially, she reached into a drawer and from beneath all its other contents drew a notebook with a black cover. It was in truth a Black Book! Here, hidden from prying eyes, my predecessor had listed all the schools regularly visited, together with names of head teachers and teachers responsible for school libraries. So far, so innocuous. But here we had both name and nature. Beside each teacher appeared descriptions, warnings. 'Difficult to get on with', 'Arrogant', 'Gushing', 'Knows little about books', 'Unco-operative'. I read with horror the damning indictments.

And of course when I made my round of the schools I was greeted with courtesy. Nothing in the Black Book tallied with my experience. It was clear enough that if my predecessor had problems with so many of her contacts . . . well, all the soldiers were out of step except Our Johnny.

Getting on with people! Almost every aspect of human affairs depends

122

upon it. Why are we still so bad at it? I address myself . . . how is it that in sixty-five years I have learned so little? Though all my life I have had the good fortune to make friends, in more superficial contacts I fail time and time again. Shy, introverted, lacking in small talk and increasingly prey to hearing problems in crowded rooms: these are my excuses. Honesty presses harder questions: charges me with insensitivity, lack of interest in other people, too much haste about my own concerns. But two useful tips at least I have picked up. When I joined the Guides as a little girl of ten I was taught to smile when out in the street. A smile from a child, they told us, often cheers a grown-up's day. (Nobody had yet thought of child-abuse, of teaching children to suspect all their elders.) I still smile in public places, and it still works; people smile back. The second lesson is more recently acquired. It goes deeper than smiling. Quakers quote often George Fox's famous injunction, 'Walk cheerfully over the world, answering that of God in every one.'

School visiting was enjoyable, but had its pitfalls. In spite of my efforts at the schools near Hawes Side, I was still naively ignorant of procedure. The general instructions were first to find a school secretary or, in primary schools which did not then employ one, the head teacher. One of my first forays as children's librarian was to a primary school built on four sides of a quadrangle. Twice round the square and I had still not located the headmaster. Lessons were in progress, no-one was about, and one must not interrupt a class. I peered more closely. At one corner of the quadrangle was a bank of bell-pushes. One was marked MASTER. Was this how to reach the headmaster? I pressed the button.

Instantly a deafening fire alarm rang out. Every door round the four walls was flung open, every class spilled into the quadrangle. I cowered in my corner, caught red-handed, not to mention red-faced with embarrassment. Yet not a word of reproach was uttered. The teachers merely commented cheerfully on the proved efficiency of their fire drill.

The end of my study course was by now in sight. It had become a way

123

of life, that continuous dogged self-discipline of organising my own studies, the completion of assignments for correspondence course dates, the annual ritual of exams. Later in life when following similar routines first for theological studies and then for an Open University degree, it was not hard to adjust to the familiar discipline. There is a sense in which I have spent the last half century compensating for my unfinished formal education. WEA classes, university extra-mural courses, summer schools, conferences, distance learning – all have been grist to my mill. Sardonically I observe that I am like Browning's grammarian: 'before living he'd learn how to live, /No end to learning.' Oh for a second life, educated, equipped, experienced!

Nothing had erased the heartache of school-leaving, the irrecoverable loss of sixth form and university life. In waking hours my thoughts seldom dwelt on it, but from the time I left school I suffered recurring night dreams of being back as a sixth form student. For twenty-five years the dreams persisted, growing ever more ludicrous as, aged twenty-something, thirty-something, nearing forty, I would sit awkwardly in a dreamworld classroom with seventeen year olds. The dreams ceased abruptly when, just forty, I became librarian of a sixth form college. At last I was, in waking fact, in the sixth form; there was no further need for dreams.

At twenty-two, however, I was eager for release from the student treadmill. My final exam was approaching. Year by year I had travelled to Manchester, usually with one or two other candidates, to sit the Library Association exams at the central library there. I liked exams. There was the day off work, the train journey, morning coffee at the Manchester Kardomah. Then in the great library the excitement of mingling with a throng in the ground floor foyer; that shiver of expectation just before opening the question paper; the race against time to get down all one knew, to round out an essay. My grades were high, not because I was brighter than other students but because exams suited my temperament.

Manchester library was an ideal venue for exam candidates. It is a circular building. The rooms used for examinations were on the outer rim of the top floor, segments of the circle with slideaway partitions between each room. At exam time the partitions were removed and an invigilator placed at each junction. In effect, this created a large exam hall accommodating perhaps hundreds of candidates, but any one of us could see only a dozen or so others. This was far less demoralising than the fearsome sight of a huge hall filled with desks.

It was the day before my last exam. I was alone in Blackpool children's library, which did not open until after school time. Behind a wooden partition was a workroom where my friend Ursula and another assistant were at their own tasks. This Ursula would be my companion and fellow candidate the following day. She was not a close friend, though we enjoyed each other's company. To Ursula I had said not one word about my feeling for Michael, though I knew that she knew.

Was she my friend? Was it kindness that prompted her, or a delicate tact; or was it, that exam eve, sheer bloody-minded cruelty?

The talk behind the screen impinged on my attention. Ursula had raised her voice. She had judged the level correctly, retaining a conversational tone as she addressed her companion, yet speaking loudly enough for every word to reach me.

'Have you heard about Michael? Seems he's got a girlfriend at long last . . . Yes, very sudden . . . But it's serious. He's already talking about getting married. I hear he met her at . . .'
The story continued. I sat like a stone. First shock and grief; I had been so sure of my man. Then anger; how could Ursula break it to me this way, on this day? She could have kept it until after the exam, then told me privately.

That evening my mother was concerned for me. In a state of acute distress, I was unable to eat and retired to my bedroom, pleading an attack of exam nerves. My mother was not deceived. She knew that exams did not prostrate me but buoyed me up. Her own teaching on self-control and the absurdity of stage fright had stood me in good stead. But I did not confide in her, neither then nor later, though for the following fortnight I fled home daily to weep and weep.

How I was to cope with the exam was the least of my problems. How, immediately, was I to face the train journey with Ursula, the whole day exclusively in her company? As it turned out, her misfortune was my salvation. Perhaps it served her right, but tragedy turned into farce and even in my misery I could see the funny side of an unexpected day.

Making my way to the railway station, I concentrated all my determination – first, not to refer in any way to what I had heard and been meant to hear, and second, not to cry. So preoccupied was I that at first I did not observe my companion's unusual jumpiness. Ursula was normally confident and capable in all situations. Soon she confessed that she had been to her doctor to ask for tranquillizers to calm her exam nerves. After some persuasion, the doctor had written the prescription, recommending that she take one the night before, one at breakfast and – only if necessary – one at lunch time, for we had exams both morning and afternoon.

It was impossible to remain angry with a friend in this state. My spirits rose slightly as hers fell. Ursula was now the vulnerable one, and my self-possession recovered. I would see her through the day. That, and the exams, would between them blank out my distress. And indeed, once in the exam room I went on to auto-pilot, became a mechanical regurgitator of information. It was a relief to escape from myself. Absorbed in writing my papers, I scarcely glanced at Ursula, but as we emerged from the exam room I could see that all was not well. She was pale, exhausted, reported that she had done badly. Worse, she was shaking.

We repaired to a café and ordered lunch. Against my advice Ursula insisted on taking a third pill, since the morning one had apparently failed her. The effect was quick, and catastrophic. I was familiar with the idiom 'She turned green', but had never actually encountered the phenomenon before. Come to think of it, I have never observed it since, either. Ursula's complexion took on a decidedly green cast. She sprawled across her chair, gasping. I summoned a waitress, and between us we propelled our patient into the ladies' loo, where she was disgustingly sick, then gently and smilingly passed out.

Quandary. I had to get back for the afternoon exam; I could not leave the insensible Ursula on the floor of a café loo. While I pondered the dilemma, however, Ursula came to – though what she came to is difficult to imagine, for her state of mind was now quite altered. The tranquillizer had worked. She was utterly relaxed, almost voluptuously euphoric. Nothing mattered, Ursula was happy. Clinging to my arm, she swayed and lurched back to the library and into the exam room. There she slumped into a chair, laid her head on the desk and closed her eyes.

Again I concentrated on my papers. From time to time I glanced towards Ursula. She appeared to have awakened, and with an expression of asinine bliss on her usually shrewd intelligent face was writing a little. Afterwards she was able to give some garbled account of what she had written. The drug-induced euphoria lasted through the afternoon, and knowing that she had done badly in the morning Ursula had taken a relaxed delight in writing whatever outrageous nonsense came into her head. She did of course fail the exam. I, to my astonishment, seemed to have done as well as usual in spite of all. The mental auto-pilot had attended to things, an internal guardian angel apparently more efficient than drugs.

After a fortnight too miserable to chronicle I felt sufficiently in control of myself to visit Michael at his branch library and to wish him happiness. It was an uneasy conversation. He contrived an awkward apology. I smiled, left him and collapsed in tears outside the library. Soon after, he secured a post in a distant county and married his lady. It was at this point that I made the worst mistake of my life.

I couldn't stand the pain, that was all. I had vowed to 'marry that man or die in the attempt' – so now death was the only option. No, not suicide. Deliberately, consciously, level headedly, I chose emotional death. From now on, if it were humanly possible, I would feel nothing. Never again, I resolved, would I be so vulnerable to hurt, never again allow that sort of unconditional commitment to another human being. I was going to cease from feeling.

It was the very reverse of my childhood promise to remember how to feel intensely. It was the negation of poetic sensibility. It was soul-death. I didn't care, I clutched at it as one in extreme pain screams for painkillers. All I wanted was not to care. I had to seek not oblivion but numb superficiality, suppressing all that ran deepest and truest in me. Now I really was the girl who runs backwards, a woman running scared.

It can be done, but the cost is terrible. With the capacity to be hurt I lost the ability to love; the inspiration to write; my religious sensitivity; my integrity. I entered a sunless place, a murky fog where all was dulled, blurred, monochrome. Alternatively, you might describe me as floating comfortably on the mere surface of quotidian ordinariness. And yes, it *was* comfortable, that drowsy absence from oneself. Had I not at nine set that alarm clock to ring at forty, I might never have awakened from self-enchanted sleep.

Only, somewhere below, something simmered. Another dream joined the recurrent back-to-sixth-form night scenario. It was a dream of Michael, from which I would wake in tears. It persisted for years, even for the first seven years of my marriage.

What nonsense all this must seem! In a world of real suffering, real cruelty, real tragedy and devastation, what price the commonplace disappointment of a silly girl? Is it even worth recounting such a sub-novelettish non-event? Perhaps it is. How many people are walking about, functioning but not feeling, in that sort of death-in-life I once voluntarily entered? Certainly I was weak and foolish, but there are many of us like that. If someone had observed my state, could the slide into half-sleep have been halted? Is it possible for us to develop the seeing eye, to be aware that even the foolish and apparently unscathed have real hurts? If such self-withdrawals could be averted, people would be free to mature; we might all enjoy a maturer society. I do not know the answer to these questions, but I contend that they are worth posing.

## *BURNING THE NOTES*

Here is my study course,
a tear-off pad of lessons –
programmed learning.
We never see the tutors
so students help each other
offering contradictory
haphazard advice.
A page a day's the system:
learn, remove and burn.
You're not allowed to keep them,
there's no revision time,
it's memorise or fail.

Burning the sheets is strange.
Hating what you do
you strike your morning match
and see what you have learnt
shrivel, flake to dust,
enter non-being.
A solemn ritual, somehow.

(Pious Hindus push out
lighted paper boats
on to holy Ganges.
In Catholic shrines you see
candles left by suppliants
guttering down to nothing.
Where is a burnt prayer?)

Yesterday's module, look:
black diagrams on white,

two-dimensional,
devoid of self-propulsion.
Watch it brown (there's colour),
writhe and curl (there's movement).
This lively element, fire,
conjures its own colour
motion and dimension
out of a death rattle.

Today's lesson, then,
that truth's not in the words
but in consuming flame?
Why then I'll catch it,
trap it between hands.

Ah no the pain!
My scorched and blistered skin!
Worse, I've killed the flame.

Those words can't have been true,
they burned away.
Nor can the flame,
my hands extinguished it.
What's truth, then, Pilate?
Branded palms,
stigmata?

## 18. First person singular, first person plural

When I was about thirteen – to backtrack for a moment – a dancing teacher who was one of my mother's friends offered to give me lessons. She can hardly have thought of starting me on ballet at that age, so perhaps it was to be tap dancing or 'modern dance'; I do not remember. My mother received this offer politely, secretly horrified at the thought of the clothes I would probably require and which she could not possibly make. Loyal to her friend, however, she put the project to me as an attractive proposition. As she afterwards admitted, mother was much relieved at my instant response: 'Oh! Must I?'

I would much rather take writing lessons, I told her – being at that time still convinced of my destiny. Since she also counted among her friends a free-lance journalist, mother agreed to sound her out. So it was that for a term or so I went weekly to Alys Myers, producing for criticism articles on whatever topics she assigned. I know I still owe much to Miss Myers' tuition and am grateful. But . . .

By the time my librarianship studies were complete, those writing lessons were seven or eight years in the past and I had no personal contact with Alys Myers, though she remained a friend of my mother's. So I was horrified when I heard about an article in a Manchester paper.

'Now studious Anne turns to dancing' was the headline; the by-line, Alys Myers. As if this were not embarrassing enough, I learned of the offending article from a reporter on the Blackpool paper, who telephoned me at the library, eager to pursue the story. Though I absolutely refused to allow any further publicity, the damage was done and there was nothing for it but to accept teasing with what good humour I could muster. For Miss Myers I am afraid I could muster none. It seemed to me a personal betrayal, to write such a piece without the subject's permission, and I fear

I told her so with some vehemence.

There was indeed a neat irony here. My new strictly-on-the-surface *persona* had forgotten or relinquished writerly ambitions. My new released-from-studies state allowed more time for social life, and among other activities I was attending a ballroom dancing class and also joining the young crowd at the Winter Gardens each Saturday night. It was one of time's more impudent reversals!

This was a waiting period. Though now properly an Associate of the Library Association I could not become a Chartered Librarian until the age of twenty-three. At that point I would be free to apply for jobs elsewhere, and intended to leave Blackpool at the earliest opportunity. Not only had I never liked the town; its penny-pinching corporation, it now appeared, refused even when I should be chartered to increase my salary to the minimum professional grading. I no longer had close friends locally, and had fretted long enough to leave the parental home.

Meanwhile I became for a year or more an unthinking gadabout, off every evening to cinema, theatre, dance hall, youth forum, dramatic society, badminton club. Uncaringly I exploited any young man who would buy me a theatre ticket, rewarding one or two with a reluctant garden-gate kiss, no more. I felt safe; if any of them got too interested, I knew I could shake him off when I left town the following year.

Who was she, this good-time girl? A butterfly emerging into light, wings still wet? So it might have appeared. Better images might be a snail creeping into her shell, an exposed worm diving hastily underground, a hedgehog rolled up to present only her defensive prickles. This was the girl who runs backwards, retreating from reality. Who was she? The young woman I look back on is a stranger whose memories I happen to inherit. Or perhaps not quite a stranger, but an acquaintance whom I recall with recognition but without intimacy. She bore my name, but Anne had slipped away. So it seems, viewed in certain lights. But this memoir is about honesty. I know that I cannot so glibly shrug off responsibility. I was that young woman. If this tale is to continue it must still be a first-person narrative.

A digression about dreams. Dreams are almost invariably first-person narratives. In a dream 'I', even if perhaps a younger 'I', am always present, usually as protagonist but at the very least as spectator. Once, however, a few years ago, before the collapse of the Iron Curtain and the Berlin Wall, I had a first-person dream in which the 'I' was someone quite other and quite unknown to me. It was as though there could be such a thing as a first-person film, where instead of being merely a viewer one actually experienced the main character's feelings: a sort of inward virtual reality.

Had I been reading about repression in eastern Europe or Stalin's Russia? Possibly. In my dream I was a woman in her forties living in some unspecified totalitarian state. She had no name. I call her Anna, since though she was not I, it was I who in the dream state was she. Anna's husband was a political dissident. She had a son and daughter, both in their teens. One night came the dreaded knock on the door, the swift search by secret police, the husband carried away. I, as Anna, suffered it all, the terror, grief, despair, anger, sheer weariness. Next I, Anna, was out shopping. Returning she, I, found the door standing open, the house ransacked. This time both children were taken. Again I experienced that whole horror, Anna's agony and devastation, the sense of falling into an abyss of pain and rage and hopelessness. It was some time after awakening before the immediacy of that experience left me.

How strange. In that dream I could experience intensely the sensations of an unknown woman, a fantasy of my subconscious mind. It is not dissimilar from the 'myself' who lived from her early twenties to late thirties; the memories of that woman's subjective experience, though undeniably mine, seem like Anna's to belong to another whose body and mind I once inhabited.

'We are legion!' shrieked the madman in the gospel story. But you don't have to be schizoid to feel plural. Serially, I seem to have lived three distinct short lives, as Young Anne, Half-asleep Anne, Mature Anne. On the other hand, concurrently – and this is a very common feeling – I have also seen myself as a number of *personae*. 'Mature Anne' was for a while quite conscious of harbouring a set of selves, some of whom were in conflict. For instance, AA librarian tended to be a conformist and AA poet a rebel. Only latterly have I reached something like a comfortable integration. Others can perhaps achieve this effortlessly, or at least in half the time. I have been a slow learner.

## MY INSIDE OUT

I pirouette in floppy floral pink,
swirl it around my thighs.
    Wouldn't you think
she'd wallow in its luxuries?
    Not she.
Today she opts for tailored pants and tie.
    How seldom we agree.

Back at the sink we roll up workday sleeves
(one each) and share an apron. No,
    we are not slaves:
she covets a kimono
    whereas I
a negligée with ribboned frippery.
    Such fractured fantasy!

My kitchen's ordered like her library,
spick as a hospital.
    Her name's Contrary Mary.
Not pleased at all,
    she's out
kicking my swept-up leaves about.
    She is my inside out.

So when she's working at her desk, ingesting
footnotes and polysyllables
    I'm fluttering
at fiction and old fables.
    She looks
scornfully at my books.
    Is that the crux?

I yawn to bed, but sister keeps me awake,
clicking her tictac brain.
    For pity's sake!
We lie there wrangling – then
remembering the alarm
sleep in each other's arm
twining our double-helix-patterned dream.

With Michael's departure my professional ambitions were at least simplified. As soon as I could claim Chartered status I would apply for a job as a children's librarian somewhere. This was a rapidly expanding specialism at that time, and I had no doubt of securing a job. Yet for Half-asleep Anne the glow had faded even from professional aspirations. All I could feel was that it didn't matter where I went, what I did, whether I succeeded. And meanwhile, inner eyes closed, I would have fun.

# 19. Fun, and deeper delight

Fun? It is not that I had not been having fun. Merely being young was fun. No, better than that: being alive is fun. Given adequate health and no more than an average modicum of anxieties, to be alive is a deep delight, an astonishing daily marvel. That conviction has remained with me, ebbing or surging according to mood and circumstance, but never extinguished.

A friend who was kind enough to assess the early chapters of this chronicle startled me by describing them as 'harrowing'. Have I been too concerned with hurts and horrors, which are perhaps more readily dramatised than those happy hours which pass unremarked? Just as for journalists most news is bad news, just as for dramatists only conflict makes a play, so perhaps for an autobiographer it is shade rather than light which delineates the picture. So let it be firmly stated, here at least: I have loved being alive, though admittedly Half-asleep Anne felt that proportionately less keenly.

If my mother is to be believed, I was a cheerful laughing baby. There are photographs of me at a few months old, smiling broadly, clearly thrilled to have arrived. Half a century later I was injured in a road accident. After two or three months confined to my bedroom, there came a day when I was carried outside by a young friend. He placed me for a few minutes in a garden chair, to feel the October wind on my face and hear it rumpling and rustling the trees. No joy could have been more intense. I was laughing with pleasure, with the sheer intoxicating fun of being on planet Earth. Now, in retirement and calmly contemplating mortality, I find life piquantly sweet. Colours, shapes, sounds, tastes and textures become richer when each day is an unmerited bonus.

How is it we have been accorded this unsolicited privilege – to be set down here, conscious among other moving objects? No wonder infants crawl off so rapidly to explore it all. No wonder painters never get over their wonder at those modulating colours. No wonder scientists are impelled to keep on discovering how it all happens.

Through many years of working with young people, it has been my chief concern to blow encouragement on sparks and embers of enthusiasm, to startle the young out of foolish fashionable boredom and rouse to flame the leaping glory of being alive. I have known sad times and low times, but never, I believe, a time when pleasure in living was blotted out. Does this accord with a girl who runs backwards? Perhaps, perhaps not. I do not claim to be consistent. Which of us is? Only inconsistent weather can create rainbows. At least I can claim to revel in rainbows.

## SWIFT RAINBOW

Wind in a winter sun
tears at the eye's tears.
Glassed with wet light bristle
Lilliput's grass spears.

Field-far the hills' haze
snow-sharpens, proud
white banners defying
crouchback cloud.

Focus of haze and light,
union of tear and dew,
sunlight and murderous cloud,
the green, the blue –

all at a stroke revealed,
cancelled, outshone:
rainbow's epiphany,
painted and gone.

Growing up is a painful and embarrassing process, but fortunately full of fun too. I enjoyed my work, my leisure; plays and films and books, friendships, dancing, outings, and not a few church activities.

Enid's roaring evangelicalism with its mission meetings and chorus-singing was no longer for me. My religious quest continued, and so did my church attendance, until at last I so stifled my soul that Half-asleep Anne felt no need of ultimate concerns. At about eighteen I had been pressed into Sunday school teaching. Our church at that time encouraged its children to sit an easy annual scripture examination, and its teachers to submit to the same not very demanding discipline. Papers were marked locally, but the best in each age group were sent to a national competition. It so happened that for the three years I entered for the junior teachers level my paper won the national prize. This allowed me three free trips to London to receive the awards, with hospitality provided.

Fun indeed! I was game for a free holiday and eager for my first experience of the capital. On the first occasion I was met and shepherded around the sights of the city by some bald avuncular gentleman from the hierarchy of the Sunday School Union. This was valuable. I learned how to negotiate the underground system and was introduced to river, tower, palace, parks, Westminster. But the constant supervision by my appointed guardian grew tiresome, and I was happier on the two later trips when I could wander alone and choose my destinations. London enthralled me – its great buildings, its bustling crowds in which one could be so blissfully anonymous, its sense of being the hub of the nation's activities. Much as I love the countryside, cities still excite me. They set something sizzling, an extra surge of adrenalin.

The third of my London adventures coincided with some special anniversary of the Sunday School Union, perhaps a jubilee; so instead of the usual large church their gathering was held in the Albert Hall, no less. On arrival I was to go straight to the Hall. Emerging from the station I was uncertain of my direction and turned back to ask a railway official. The reply in voluble Cockney might as well have been in Finno-Ugric. I retreated, baffled. In the street, however, I encountered a police officer. They were about, in those days. As a child I had been taught to 'ask a policeman', and now was the time to practise the lesson. The officer, at once recognising my accent, asked where in Lancashire I came from.

'Blackpool? I'm from Lancaster myself. Good to hear a northern voice. Come on, I'll walk with you. What's on at the Albert Hall, then?'

His reaction to my explanation was one of astonished amusement. Casting an appreciative eye over me, the young constable exclaimed, 'You don't look like a Sunday school teacher!'

Stereotypes, stereotypes. If I had told him I was also a librarian, would he have been even more startled?

Inside the Albert Hall it was my turn to be amazed. Never had I seen so large a gathering, so immense an indoor venue. Faces at the far end of the Hall were pinheads. But soon I was swept into an ante-room with the other prize winners, one from each age group. Most were children with their parents. Only one was older than me, the winner of the senior teachers' award. Stewards formed us into an ordered queue, youngest first. Our prizes were to be handed to us by a royal personage, and we had to cross the stage in turn to receive them. Receive with the left, shake hands with the right, was the instruction. At the last moment, a further command ran down the line, applying to female candidates only.

'Curtsey to the duchess. Pass it on: curtsey to the duchess!'

Hearing the whisper approaching, I felt I was in Alice's Wonderland, and had much ado to stifle my giggles.

After the event, my hosts claimed me and ushered me away to supper and bed; but the following day was all my own. Part of it I spent at Windsor, I remember, having 'done' the chief tourist attractions in the city on my two previous visits. I retain a picture of a young girl in a crisp flower-sprigged white piqué dress, striding through Windsor main street and up to the castle: twenty-one, grown-up at last and free as the summer breeze.

I gazed over the view from the castle, soaked in the beauty, the history, the nearness of London; talked to other tourists, acquired a boyfriend for an afternoon. Preoccupied with England's history, I was more truly bubbling with hopes for the future.

The same feelings suffuse my memory of the Festival of Britain. Still staggering to its economic feet after the war, in 1951 Britain set about restoring its own morale and at the same time advertising its wares to the world. The Festival of Britain was to rival the Victorian Great Exhibition. Not only would new buildings transform the south bank of London's river; every town and village in the land should be involved. Street parties were planned, musical events, plays and pageants and artworks to celebrate Britain's past, present and future. The whole nation would have a party.

It was my good fortune to attend one of these events. I happened to be spending a holiday with friends in Hitchin, Hertfordshire. What Hitchin is like today I have no idea. Has it like so many small towns become a sprawling undistinguished collection of housing estates and chainstores? In 1951 it was a modest market town. An old castle stood on a low eminence above an open field through which a stream ran under a small bridge. This was the setting for the local Festival pageant, and tiers of spectator seating were erected. From here – I occupied a privileged visitor's position on the front row – we watched medieval knights in armour gallop down from the castle on colourfully caparisoned horses, across the stream and into the acting area. The town's history unfolded, a microcosm of a romanticised England.

And then the accession of a young queen added a fine spumy crest to the wave of optimism. 'The new Elizabethan age' was the phrase in every newspaper, a new era with scope for freedom, enterprise, endeavour, success. My mother and father and I with a dozen more neighbours squashed into someone's living room and sat agog before what was to be the new idol of the age. This was the only television set accessible to us. It occupied a perch high above eye level, so that all could see the tiny screen even if the details were unclear to those at the back of the room. There rode our heroine in her (black and white) golden coach, actually at that very moment approaching her crowning. There was the great Abbey, reduced to ten inches.

'Vivat! Vivat Regina Elisabeta!' We watched and listened, rapt in wonder at this new technological magic, thrilled with an unquestioned devotion to queen and country. The Festival and the Coronation: perhaps these were the last delicious tastes of a corporate English innocence, though few will have recognised that at the time. Not I, certainly. I was entranced by the magic of yesterday, the fun of today, the hope of tomorrow.

Mind you, at that time I was still intending to marry Michael.

# 20. What next?

An organism which is not growing is dying. True, we are all dying, in the sense of the remorseless life cycle which propels us towards the end. 'Time held me green and dying', as Dylan Thomas described his younger self. Yet until the end, or near it, we can be growing too. Even after I so deliberately chose emotional death, there was growth of sorts, however stunted. And the potential for healthier growth remained, dormant. In later years I was able to change and develop.

The previous chapters depicted an ignorant and not untypical child of her time. Politically naive, unblinkingly patriotic and monarchist, still believing in the sanctity of English history as it was then presented: how could that young woman become the writer of this page, who is a moderate republican, left of centre, mortified by much that the English have done to their nearest neighbours and to the rest of the world? And how could a fervent teenage evangelical turn eventually into a postmodern post-Christian, albeit one still deeply concerned with the spiritual quest? Only though growth.

This is why, though tempted daily to pessimism by the state of the earth and its peoples, I am at the same time partly an optimist. Growth is possible, consciousness can be raised, understanding can be reached. I have seen it happen in other individuals. It is also a social process, although we can no longer accept the nineteenth century view of inevitable progress. Nothing is inevitable, neither progress nor disaster. But only look! There have been great movements of concern in the twentieth century, inconceivable to most of our ancestors: declarations of human rights; environmental consciousness; upgrading the worth of previously devalued people – women, black people, the disabled. We may not be living up to our ideals, but aspiration must always precede practice. Though there are many to lament the loss of morality in today's society, our species in fact is still in the remarkable human business of creating values. If you doubt that, think briefly of . . . well, here are some random instances: the Inquisition; Bedlam; witch-hunting; child labour in factories; lives lived in acute terror of hellfire or demonic spirits; slavery.

Most of my own learning has taken place late in life. Minds are elastic, flexible, and like muscles can become more so when exercised. In theory, then, it might be argued that with the now increased human lifespan we should have a lot of wiser individuals and collectively a wiser society. There is little evidence of that, for a number of reasons. One reason would be the strength of those opposing forces, inertia and fear of change. These forces tighten their grip as we get older (a fact not unconnected with diminution of physical energy) and so make for inflexibility.

I have changed, and will change. I have learned, and I hope will go on learning. This memoir is partly a reminder of the process and a spur to it. There may also be some encouragement for others anxious about what they perceive as unteachable stupidity, whether in individuals or societies. The human race has the capacity to grow up, however slow and painful its past and present meanderings through toddlers' tantrums and teenage intransigence. The well known ethologist Konrad Lorenz, considering the course of evolution, explains why in spite of all he can remain an optimist.

'I know from reckoning in geologic measurements of time that we humans have only just recently been anthropoid apes; I know, in addition, about the dangers for the human soul that have been precipitated by the rapid development of the human mind; and I know something more: that many of these dangers are caused, quite unambiguously, by sicknesses that are, at least in principle, curable.' (The Waning of Humaneness, Unwin Hyman 1988, original German 1983)

But to return to the chronicle . . . In 1951 my father turned seventy. He had not worked for many years, though occasionally undertaking minor auditing commissions for small businesses. For some years his health had been poor, and he was reduced to passive dependence on my mother – emotionally, financially, and for decision making. Possibly he was often depressed; I doubt if I would have recognised that. I am unwilling to describe the man as I saw him. There is no point in cataloguing the faults of one long gone, and I am uneasily aware that the young judge harshly. My mother tried to defend him, tried to make me understand how humiliating it was for a man not to be the family breadwinner.

That James Henry doted upon Emma was clear, and unsurprising. That she remained so affectionately attached to him always surprised me, but it was undoubtedly the case. Whatever the deficiencies of my upbringing, the small household was full of love, with both parents devoted to one another and to me. That, for a child, must be of first importance.

His seventieth birthday seemed to deal the *coup de grâce* to James Henry. Virtually overnight, he ceased to struggle with life. He became recognisably an old man. Madame, on the other hand, was at the peak of her career. She was in constant demand as speaker, chairwoman, reciter; taught in the mornings in small private schools, in the afternoons received private pupils in her hired studio. She was normally out when I returned from work, so it would be my duty to give my father his tea. It was little enough; my mother prepared the meals, saw to washing, shopping and the rest, and often had to nurse my father through painful illness. She herself was never unwell. It never occurred to me that she was under any strain.

Both of them delighted in my small professional successes and encouraged me to apply for jobs. My first try was for a position in London, in the borough of Acton. The metropolis, as I had glimpsed it on those visits, allured me, and the notion of living within reach of all that London offered was attractive.

All expenses for an interview would be paid, so I booked a night at a good hotel and, on the train, took my seat in the dining car for a luxury meal. This was the life! I was, as mentioned, having fun. The following morning, with a hearty hotel breakfast inside, I set off for Acton. Though the interview was not until afternoon, I meant to spend the morning exploring the area and the library. I did – and was thoroughly disappointed. A dreary seedy district, a cramped old-fashioned library: this was not where I hoped to further my career. I decided therefore that I did not want the job and must simply make sure I was not offered it.

There were two other candidates on the short list, and as both had specialist certificates which I had not yet acquired I felt confident of rejection. Nor did I strive to impress the interviewing board, though being truthful by nature I gave no false answers. Being in no anxiety about acquitting myself well, I enjoyed the interview with detached amusement. One man quizzed me at length about Blackpool, and I quickly realised that he had an agenda of his own; he wanted statistics of population and municipal spending to compare with Acton's.

Then came the blow. I was recalled; I was chosen. It was necessary to stammer out a tactful refusal, rather to the surprise and dismay of the panel. My problem was, I already knew, that no expenses would be paid to one who refused their offer. So much for the lavish railway dinner and fine hotel! On these I had expended much of my month's salary, and that excellent breakfast was now many hours ago. It would be many more hours before I reached home, but this time all I dared to eat on the train was an apple and a Mars bar. Lesson: never attend an expensive interview unless you want the job! I was amused, mildly inconvenienced, and quite unworried. There would be other posts to apply for.

I was gliding over the surface of life, two-dimensionally; hiding from hurt, having fun. One evening at the ballroom dancing class already referred to, the fun grew fast and frenzied. A Gay Gordons was in progress, and my partner was a newcomer who had already been the centre of mirth for his inability either to keep time to music or to direct his feet as the teacher instructed. He had at least grasped that The Gay Gordons should be danced skipping; so, feet flailing wildly, he grasped me in a furious stampede, trampling my feet and eventually clearing the small dance floor as all the other couples took evasive action. We finished, the two of us, in a hysterical heap in the middle of the floor. This apparently crazy young man recovered himself sufficiently to apologise for his clumsiness and, to make amends, insisted on seeing me home, despite opposition from another would-be escort.

My partner's name was Trevor. He was a grocer, and the following day was the Grocers Ball. Trevor had taken it into his head to learn to dance: yes, in one lesson, and the night before. Now he suggested that I should partner him at the ball. He had two tickets, he told me; though it later transpired that he had only his own, and had much ado the following morning to acquire a second.

For a lark, I agreed, and was ready in what finery I possessed when he called to collect me. In the street, however, I was startled to discover that we were not going by bus or tram but that Trevor had his own transport. I think I had not then ridden in a car more than three times, and certainly did not dream of any friend of mine possessing such a thing. (During a stay with Eileen and her Air Force husband, the latter had propounded his theory that light vertical-take-off mini-planes would be available to ordinary citizens before the motor car became general!) To be accurate, this was not a car but a grocer's delivery van, and that of venerable age. 1930: older than me! I surveyed the vehicle with distaste and some alarm. Was I to sit in that, in my lovely ballgown? The 'lovely ballgown' was a cheap confection of rayon and velveteen, but nonetheless precious. The look I cast was not lost on Trevor, as he later told me. The van was a Ford called Jezebel and was his mistress, his passion. It was a case of 'love me, love my van', but I had absolutely no intention of loving either.

At the Grocers Ball Trevor and I were at pains to pass ourselves off as better acquainted than we were. It created a sort of bond, a shared amusing secret. And indeed we became acquainted. Jezebel, I discovered, had her advantages. Trevor loved to drive, and took me to wonderful countryside otherwise inaccessible to me. Like me, he loved lakes and mountains, trees and waterfalls. In town we frequented cinemas, coffee bars. The coffee bar, with its new-fangled *espresso* machines and equally new club sandwiches, was at that time the gathering ground for young people. The age of drugs and alcohol had definitely not arrived.

I liked Trevor. He was generous, he was fun, he was anxious to please. He was kind, and all too soon this kindness was to be my vital support. It emerged that he was a partial invalid. Through the summer he suffered from severe prostrating asthma, in the winter from a skin disease which was part of the same syndrome. Thus I was sorry for him too. I could not love him, and told him so when pressed, even told him about Michael. And I made it clear that the friendship would be short-lived, for I would shortly be leaving Blackpool. On these terms, I was happy to enjoy his company. If I was exploiting Trevor, it was, I hope, openly and without pretence. But I had reckoned without the persistence of my suitor.

## 21. Mill chimneys

And after all, jobs were not cherries for the picking. Where were the advertisements which had so tantalised me while I waited to become chartered? Suddenly no-one in those desirable locations – great cities, historic towns, green counties – seemed to want a children's librarian. I was disinclined to wait, had waited long enough. The first suitable job to present itself was in Rochdale, and I took it. I had no difficulty in securing the post, for those years doing librarian's work for assistant's pay had the benefit of providing me with useful experience. Again I was to be in charge of a central children's library, this time with responsibility also for children's provision at branch libraries. Again I was required to visit the local schools, this time more often and to provide systematic practical support.

The month's notice required by Blackpool was enough, I supposed, for me to find digs in Rochdale, but this proved not so simple. Used to the shifting population of a seaside town, where lodgings and bedsits abound, I was unprepared for a very different kind of community. In Blackpool everyone seemed to have 'come from' somewhere else, or their parents had. In Rochdale the population was static, all seemed to have grown up there and their progenitors before them. To take on outside workers was unusual. I was the only one on the library staff whose home was elsewhere. Little need, then, for furnished apartments.

Trevor, keen not to lose touch with me in spite of my declared intentions, offered his services. He would drive me round Rochdale on a tour of the half dozen addresses we had managed to glean from the local paper. We went, not in Jezebel but in his father's car, a respectable black saloon.

At every address but one I drew a blank. Every room was taken. The exception caused us some merriment. The landlady at first seemed reluctant to admit me. The room was hardly suitable, she said, for a young lady like me. A puzzling remark, but desperation made my pleas more urgent, and the woman agreed that I could view the room.

'I'll just tell my companion that I'm coming in,' I said, turning towards Trevor who was still in the car. The landlady reacted with horror.

'Is that the police?' she snapped. Police cars were black in those days. By the time I summoned words to deny this unexpected misconception, the door had been slammed in my face. Later, colleagues told me that this particular street was notorious for houses of ill repute.

The day had proved a wild goose chase. Some way had still to be found of securing accommodation. I appealed to the minister of my church, asking him to contact a minister of a Rochdale church who might know someone kind enough to take me in. The minister concerned passed the letter to his wife, who in turn read it out at her women's meeting. But it was not one of her flock who answered the call.

Miss Hartley, a retired office worker and one of the great spinster brigade, was one who 'kept herself to herself.' She had only one friend, and lived a circumscribed life. Turned seventy, Miss Hartley had perhaps begun to recognise what she would never have admitted, that life was passing her by. That New Year Miss Hartley had made a serious resolution. Whatever might be the first opportunity to present itself that year, she would seize it. January had passed without event. It was now February, and it happened that Miss Hartley, a staunch Anglican, one day reluctantly allowed herself to be persuaded to accompany her nonconformist friend to the chapel women's meeting. That was the day the letter was read aloud.

A young professional woman required a place to stay, at least temporarily. Was this the chance she must seize, pondered Miss Hartley? She who so closely guarded her privacy, was she to open her home to some unknown girl? But she was a woman of her word, even though the promise had only been made to herself.

Miss Hartley was tall, firmly erect, neat and brisk and very efficient. She had a shrewd intelligence and a rather prim expression which could soften into kindness. Her stern eyes could, I discovered, twinkle merrily with amusement and even mischief. During my first month with her, however, she alarmed me with a sudden frostiness. The occasion was this.

I began to feel unwell, and having not yet registered with a doctor in Rochdale I took sick leave and fled to see my doctor in Blackpool. The problem was simply that the change of abode had upset my menstrual cycle and the doctor had to prescribe something to bring on an overdue period. When I returned two days later and explained this to Miss Hartley her manner noticeably stiffened. It was clear that she thought I was pregnant and had taken advantage of my employers' gullibility and her kindness to get away from home. When, within a week, all was demonstrably well, my landlady relaxed. From that day until her death, I was her girl.

Not that there was any sentiment about Miss Hartley. She took me in hand with some severity, deploring what she regarded as the sloppy upbringing which had left me at twenty-three culpably ignorant about domestic matters. The moment I returned from work each evening, Miss Hartley would begin. Before I could even remove my coat or sit down, the monologue would erupt.

'Now Anne, I've been waiting for you to come home. I must tell you at once while it's fresh in my mind, what I've been doing today and how I've done it. You need to know this.'

Then would follow a lengthy lecture, perhaps with demonstration, on her day's domestic chores: how she had washed curtains, cleaned brasses, baked a cake, sewn a pillowslip or whatever it might be. My days off became practical lessons in housewifery, and little by little I began to enjoy it all. I owe much to Miss Hartley's detailed tuition.

## *THE MISS H's*

They both had steel hair
and a kind of kindness,
my early mentors.

Miss Heaton's bony fingers grasped our shoulders,
forced us to office stools.
'Sit, girl. You'll spend enough of your working life
standing.' She stood.
'And leave your work in order every night
so someone else could deal with it,' she warned.
'You might be under a bus.'

The day came when I was under a bus.
Thanks, Miss Heaton.

She and Miss Hartley: what a generation.
Born before 1900,
possible husbands quenched in mud and gas,
they grew strong sinews,
used elbow grease for scrubbing –
floors, fol-de-rols, hankies and sentiment.

Miss Hartley had no nieces.
'No one,' she told me crisply,
'will deal with things. I have to do it myself,
get organised beforehand.
All the bedding's clean.
I've burned my love letters.
Been to the cemetery today: the grave's
ordered and paid for.'

Thanks, Miss Hartley.
I file my papers now, from lifelong habit,
and wash the cups at night.
I won't be a lot of trouble when I go,
although I liked it here.
You showed me how to like it,
striding along your favourite beauty spot,
Rochdale canal.

I liked knowing you both,
Miss H, Miss H.

When I first began the hunt for digs, an acquaintance who knew
Rochdale surprised me with a warning. 'Mind you get somewhere with a
bathroom.' Never having encountered a house without a bathroom (even
my grandfather had one) I took this as a joke. It was not. The typical
house in that town of textile mills was built before the need of bathrooms
for mill workers was dreamt of. In Rochdale houses were praised for
durability, not for refinements like bathrooms and gardens. 'A good stone
built house' was a common term of approval. Miss Hartley had installed
her own tiny bathroom only the year before my arrival. She lived in a
Victorian terrace of 'two up two down' houses in the quaintly named
Overt Street. This was simply Lancashire-speak: over t'street. Other local
names included Top o'th'Hill and Well i'th'Lane. They reflected the all-
pervasive local accent.

In the two years I spent in Rochdale, I never became accustomed to the ubiquitous mean streets of squalid-looking, though trimly kept, industrial age housing, each dwelling opening directly on to the street. The town centre was admittedly fine, with a town hall of Victorian Gothic grandeur, a parish church atop a breathtaking flight of steps, a wide square and a steep well-landscaped park through which I walked to work, for the library stood there also. The back wall of the library descended sheer into the murky mysteries of Rochdale canal. It has since been culverted, but in those days the smell of that open canal was an olfactory sensation of unpleasant intensity. No doubt it carried effluent from a score of factories. I regret to say that from the staffroom window we would throw our kitchen waste directly into this filthy conduit.

Nor was smell the only pollutant. With a forest of mill chimneys disgorging their soot, the whole town was bathed in black. Given enough rain to wet the pavements, you were walking in black treacle. On fine days when washing was hung out, it would be brought in covered in black smuts. Never during those two years were my fingernails properly clean. Petticoat hems were grey with a grime that no washing could erase.

How could one have imagined that it was almost the end of an era? Later the looms fell silent, the workers became unemployed. Factory windows were boarded up, then buildings demolished. The great chimneys were dismantled. A few years ago one mill engineer who had made a second career as an industrial archaeologist was interviewed for radio, standing in one of the few specimens of such chimneys still extant. I listened in fascination.

# A SMALL ROOM

'This is the smallest room in Rochdale,' said
the engineer turned archaeologist
stepping into a chimney. With a twist
of arm and neck, a craning of the head
he indicated skywards, where a disk
of daylight proved the tube was limited.

'Six feet across, two hundred and seventy high.
It doesn't look as tall as that from here,
seeing it foreshortened. If the sky is clear
you'd guess at fifty feet – but you'd deny
the scale of it. Things aren't what they appear.
The builders didn't court eternity

and tops of some have fallen, but at base
they take some demolition. Would you think
that round us now the wall's sixteen feet thick
in all directions? – tapering, as you'd guess,
till at the top it's less than a three brick
cladding that opens into emptiness.'

We live in a small room. All hunch at night
within six feet, rehearsing what's to come.
It's dark, it's stifling. Yet we dream of home,
locating it beyond that disk of light,
deceptive in its distance. One small room
more firmly built than prisons. Is it right

to tilt the head and gaze at dubious sky?
Or truer just to pound the walls and cry?

To live in Rochdale in the 1950s was for me a revelation of the pride a close-knit working class community took in its work, its worth, its sense of belonging. I had no wish to spend my life there, but appreciated that warm community spirit. Are there still such places? I doubt it. All the conditions for that kind of rootedness in a single locality, the security of a staple industry, are gone. I am glad to have known it once.

# 22. Power, and powerlessness

Waste paper bins overflowed, sacks were filled. My first days at work were spent recklessly purging the accumulated administrative dross of years. Jack, the technical assistant whose services were partly at my disposal, was thrilled if a little scared by my abandon. Jack had held the fort during the interim between my predecessor's departure and my arrival, and had not ventured to alter anything. As he talked me through the systems those first three days Jack's eyes grew wide and wider at my cavalier orders. 'Don't need it, get rid of it,' was my reaction to the clutter of unnecessary records. I was energetically new-brooming, seizing power.

Jack was a pleasure to work with and we at once established a happy relationship. There was attraction between us, never strong enough on either side to tempt us to become more than colleagues. It was some time before I discovered that though only in his twenties Jack had already been married and deserted by his wife, and was embarking on divorce proceedings. I hope he lived happily ever after, but who does? He was seldom uncheerful and always a staunch support to me.

For the delectation of young readers, the children's library provided a goldfish tank. This, rather to my relief, was very much Jack's personal prerogative. I was more than happy to leave the messy and difficult business of cleaning and renewing the tank to him. An amused spectator, I enjoyed his lengthy struggles to catch those elusive slithery fish before the tank could be emptied. It was Jack's personal pleasure to spend his half day on the moors, combing tarns for the water weeds and little live creatures that would keep his goldfish comfortable. I was glad of Jack's strong muscles, too, when we had large consignments of books to pack and deliver to schools.

I was often out of the library, visiting branches and schools, and so

157

came to know the town well. One of the more demanding tasks, and certainly the most rewarding of my stay in Rochdale, was helping to design, equip and stock a newly built secondary school library. Since the public library was connected also with the art gallery and museum service, work could occasionally be diversified. One week we held a folk-museum exhibition, staffed by the senior members of the library staff, where I thoroughly enjoyed taking command and airing my limited knowledge of the history of the town and domestic lifestyles. Then there were luxury days, when booksellers would send a car to collect me and whirl me away to Manchester, Preston, Huddersfield or Lytham, to be wined and dined in the hope of lucrative orders. Children's film shows, tied to promoting the pleasures of reading, occupied some evenings, as did talks to local adult groups.

Besides Jack, the services of a junior assistant were also at my disposal. These young people came to me on a rotation basis, just as I had been deployed in my junior year. For the first time, I was in a position to give orders, and enjoying it.

Power, independence, a clean slate. It was a slight irritation to me that I seemed powerless after all to shrug off the attentive Trevor. Rochdale was within travelling distance of Blackpool, even in those slow pre-motorway days, and he took a mischievous delight in hurtling over the moors at Jezebel's maximum speed. Likewise I could spend Sundays in Blackpool, and increasingly yielded to persuasion to do so.

I didn't intend it, but I didn't care enough to stop it. After Michael, nothing really mattered. Where I went, who I went with, where I lived, whether I married, were matters of indifference. And there was undeniably a certain *cachet* in having arrived in Rochdale already equipped with a boyfriend and the social standing that (absurdly) conferred. I wanted, in so far as I had the strength to want anything, to be an independent career woman. Contrariwise, and I was contrary foolish, I was increasingly aware of the social pressures of the age.

A group of female junior assistants were giggling together in the staffroom. They were aged sixteen, seventeen. I overheard Evelyn.

'If I haven't got a wedding ring on my finger by the time I'm twenty-two, I'll know I'm really on the shelf.' Then, noticing me, she blushed. 'Oh, sorry, Anne, nothing personal.' I suppose at twenty-four I seemed old to her. I was not, I was immature and vulnerable to pressure, even Evelyn's.

My mother too was perhaps similarly torn. She certainly had her doubts about my wisdom, though carefully said nothing that might harden folly into resolve. Tiptoeing delicately, she did enquire what Trevor's interests were.

'Well . . . er . . . cars, you know, and driving,' was my somewhat sheepish reply. Trevor's letters and conversations were much filled with the hours he spent on the garage floor underneath his temperamental beloved and the line of vans and cars that succeeded her. My mother did not pursue the point, beyond a look that conveyed much: that raised eyebrow, that Madame-ish sardonic half smile. On the other hand, she clearly hoped to see me married, and to someone who would provide that 'real home' of which she had too often spoken.

Trevor was at pains to make himself useful and agreeable to my parents, and indispensable to me. Agreeable he was. Against my will and judgment I grew fond of him, pitied him when he was ill, had not the heart to bring the relationship to a halt though I often planned to. It became assumed by all, including ourselves, that we would marry. I tried to persuade myself that I was in love; but it didn't matter too much, I was Half-asleep Anne, not really feeling, coasting along and letting life carry me.

We became engaged. It was my initiative as much as Trevor's. Security. Status. The power of the ring. A sense that
> Love, mere love, is beautiful indeed
> And worthy of acceptation

159

as Elizabeth Barrett Browning put it. Gratitude. Affection. Were these all unworthy motives? Trevor endeared himself to my parents by calling, not to request their daughter's hand exactly, but at least to make a formal declaration of intent to my father in old-time style.

The segment of myself that was still awake knew that a mistake was being made. Half-asleep Anne shrugged. If Trevor wanted me so much, why shouldn't he get what he wanted? For sheer persistence he deserved to have his own way, and for his undoubted kindness. Even so, I think I would not have gone through with it but for what happened next. I needed that kindness, I needed the loving and businesslike support that Trevor and his parents provided. After that, my obligation and gratitude made retraction impossible. I quelled the qualms and set myself determinedly to love this man and to become a new person, a suitable wife for him.

A new person . . . who was I then? In the first months in Rochdale I was still in the business of enjoying my job, having fun in my leisure time, and trying not to ask myself awkward questions. With soul-shutters closed, my spiritual awareness died. Occasionally I went to Trevor's church (he was loosely a Methodist) but my religion was now skin deep only. He had no interest in poetry, and I had no urge to write it. I began to read women's magazines, the only period of my life when they have appealed to me. I was shrinking, and that tiny beleaguered remnant of full consciousness knew it. But then, as my son confirms from his own experience, we reinvent ourselves more than once in a lifetime.

## NOT A POEM

This is a pencil. Yes.
No doubt of that.
And here are fingers holding it, and this
a blank sheet.

Not quite. Four or five lines
already sketched.
Poems and other hieroglyphic signs
need to be watched –

they grow so rapidly
and hide so much.
Glance sharply round and whistle carelessly.
Who's on the watch?

Does anyone suspect
that poetry's
a cover to obscure a furtive act?
the truth is

I need the pencil, see,
to finish off
drawing myself. I blur off helplessly.
I'm just a rough

gingerbread shape without
extremities
except for hands to grip the pencil that
somehow tries

to get the picture done.
But I pretend
I'm here already, firm and fully drawn.
I gaze around,

tap out a rhythm, try
to be casual.
No-one must know it isn't poetry.
Me, above all.

## 23. Emma Cleator: the end and the beginning

The phone call reached me at the library. 'Come at once, mother unconscious after a fall.' I hastened to Blackpool.

Madame was at that time teaching part-time in a small private school. It appeared that she had fallen down a flight of stairs there and had not recovered consciousness. Why not? What had made her fall? No-one knew.

She lay like a huge mound, inert behind the cot sides of a high hospital bed. Swathed anonymously in a shapeless hospital gown, she seemed scarcely a person, let alone my indomitable mother. Tests revealed a cerebral haemorrhage. Presumably this had occurred at the top of the stairs; but again, why? A fit woman at the peak of her career, she had not succumbed to illness for years.

It was January 1956. In about a month Emma would be 57, yet her hair was scarcely grey and her face unlined. Though she always considered herself plain, deprecating her size and her thin wispy hair, her face had in fact a rare beauty. Perhaps it was as much the intense attraction of her expression, as any feature, that held people enthralled. Eyes bright blue, intelligent yet tender; mouth and eyebrows mobile as any actress – it was a beauty that defies analysis and description. Now it was erased. The features remained, the personhood was absent.

My father was bewildered, unable to act. Trevor took charge, ferrying us daily to hospital. At this time my parents had rooms in a pleasant suburban house, the home of elderly sisters. A bedroom was made available for me, and I settled into the role of my father's housekeeper, seeing to meals and washing and such routine matters. The landladies were concerned and kind. One taught me a little cookery. The other had been a keen embroideress but could no longer see well enough to continue her craft. She gave me her immense collection of silks, many of which I still have and use. But as the days dragged on their anxiety sharpened, became less altruistic.

The coma did not lift. Sometimes the patient was restless, flinging her heavy body alarmingly against the cot rails, flailing unco-ordinated arms and legs. Still or active, she was totally unresponsive. Then one day she surfaced. It was a fleeting flicker of consciousness, but long enough for Emma to realise that we were with her.

Trevor stood on one side of the bed, I on the other. She had been quiet that day and the cot sides were lowered. Realising, I suppose, that it was my hand that held hers, mother made what was clearly a huge effort. Dragging my hand towards Trevor, she said simply, 'Trevor . . . take this . . .' Trevor took my hand and hers. Almost immediately she was lost to us, lost to herself. Only once after that did we hear her voice. She was not, that time, fully conscious, more like one in a frenzied nightmare. I can never erase from my memory that wild shriek of despair.

'Sake of Anne! Sake of Anne!' It rang penetratingly through the ward.

Six words. Into those six words were packed a quarter century of stress, privation, self control that had become self-repression. At last she had snapped. Not yet fully understanding, I yet felt a piercing knowledge of the heart. Then, almost following mother's example as she slipped into oblivion, I became numb, an automatic Half-asleep Anne.

She would not recover, they told me. Death would be soon – days or hours. It was to me the doctor and sister spoke. My father's wits had left him; he seemed unable to take in anything that was said. Emma's death was a notion he was simply not equipped to contain. She was his life support system, it was unthinkable that he could be long without it.

It was three weeks after the haemorrhage when the end came. Prompted by the sister, Trevor and I sat all night in the ward, noting wryly that it was our first night together. Towards dawn death was confirmed, though to our perceptions there had been no change in the lifeless mass that was Emma's body. I felt nothing, no twinge of grief; shed no tears, even indulged in a sort of unseemly levity which, rightly, shocked my fiancé. The girl was running backwards.

Still, there was much to be done, and with Trevor's help I did it: cremation to arrange, death to register, papers to sort, people to apprise. Madame's school and all her private pupils had to be told, as well as her friends and her one remaining brother. Meanwhile I had already been three weeks absent from work, and was needed in Rochdale. But what was to become of James Henry? That question could not be long deferred, but certain immediate practicalities came first.

Gathering his last shreds of sanity, my shattered father pocketed the necessary documents and allowed me to shepherd him to the registrar's office. That functionary, correctly dealing with the widower rather than the daughter, stationed me at the back of the room and addressed himself to James Henry, who answered abstractedly with 'Yes . . . yes' as required. It was when the registrar recapitulated certain necessary dates that I broke in.

'No, no!' I interposed, actually laughing. 'There's a mistake there. What was the wedding date?'

'It's correct,' insisted the registrar, and with a firm 'Not now' and a meaningful gesture commanded me to silence.

13th February 1952. Four years previously. What sort of a date was that? My mind was seething with bewilderment and incipient anger. I had long assumed that I was not J.H. Roe's daughter, but my parents had always passed as a married couple. As we walked home I mercilessly bombarded the nearly speechless widower with questions. To only one did I get a clear answer.

'Whose daughter am I?'

'Mine.'

I would rather have heard almost any other answer.

Now, when marriage has become an optional extra and parentage loose and interchangeable, it is difficult to imagine how essential was the marital state among the *petit bourgeoisie* of that time. It had in fact never occurred to me that the so-called Mr and Mrs Roe were not married, and I was deeply angry that my mother had never seen fit to tell me the real state of affairs. My rights as a grown-up daughter had, I felt, been slighted. And now, who could answer my questions? For a start, what was my name?

Accompanied by Trevor, I hurried next day to the registrar. As soon as he was free I was admitted.

'Yes, I was expecting you,' said the registrar disarmingly. 'You had a shock yesterday, I could see.'

I had my birth certificate with me. It was not the original, but a copy procured by my mother when I required one on starting work: a brief version with no mention of parentage. The original was lost, my mother had said at the time; and I now recalled the confused embarrassment it had seemed to occasion her. The original was not lost; I found it later among her papers.

'This is my fiancé,' I explained, insisting on Trevor's presence. 'We plan to be married next year, and I need to know my legal name.'

The registrar explained that if a man admits paternity the child may bear his name, and I was indeed Anne Watson Roe. There was no evading it. James Henry Roe was in truth my biological father, for whom I now had responsibility. I was in a cold, furious despair.

This was not alleviated when I found among Emma's papers a letter addressed to me. It had been written on my eighteenth birthday and was to be opened only at her death. Instead of the explanation I now expected, this turned out to be simply a loving maternal keepsake, intended to be treasured in memory of its writer. To my lifelong shame and sorrow, I have to record that in my foolish anger I burned the letter after only a single reading. What would I give now to reclaim those words?

It is now time to introduce my uncle. Robert Shadbolt Cleator was the youngest of John Alfred's children. He and Emma, offspring of the second marriage, were considerably younger than their half-brothers and very close throughout their childhood. Since there were many Roberts in the extended Cleator family and all the variants (Rob, Robbie, Bob, Bert) were in use, this one was called by part of his second name, my grandmother's maiden name, Shadbolt. He was Shad.

My mother spoke often of Shad, in affectionate reminiscence, but we seldom saw him though he still lived in Fleetwood. According to mother, this was because she would have no dealings with Shad's wife Doris. Of this Doris my mother spoke slightingly, indeed snobbishly, describing her as a vulgar barmaid whom Shad had inadvisedly picked up and whom we (heavens, who were We?) did not wish to know. Shad became a fish buyer on the Fleetwood docks, and very occasionally would arrive on half-hour visits ('Doris doesn't know') with a welcome parcel of fresh fish. On my twenty-first birthday he gave me a generous £21, enough to buy a good quality bicycle. I had the impression that Shad was mildly fond of me. Childless himself, he seemed rather to relish having a niece, though he had not figured in my childhood at all.

Shad came to the funeral, and I pressed him for explanations. With some reluctance he allowed that Trevor and I might visit.

We were received politely but without my uncle's usual cordiality.

'For a start,' began Mrs Cleator tartly, 'you are not to call your uncle "Shad". It's disrespectful not to say "Uncle". And his name is Robert. Uncle Robert to you. And *my* name is not Doris. It's Doreen. Aunt Doreen, please, or Mrs Cleator.'

It soon became clear that Aunt Doreen/Doris held my mother in as much contempt as Madame had held her. Education and professional ability weighed less than nothing in Aunt's scales, comfortably heavy with her own life of marital probity. Shad made no effort to defend his sister, but agreed to answer my questions.

The story was commonplace enough. Emma had become acquainted with an older, married man, an accountant living near Fleetwood and commuting to Bury on a train she frequently used herself. Professing an interest in elocution, James Henry became Miss Cleator's pupil, taking lessons in her home, my grandfather's house. Shad one day entered the house to find the pair enjoying sexual delights on the parlour settee. (The one with the sacrosanct painted velvet cushions, I wondered?). Emma fell pregnant, but as she was large of build the pregnancy did not show until its later stages, whereupon Emma discreetly withdrew to a home for unmarried mothers in Blackpool, until after the birth. The infant was put into foster care with a family named Watson and only reclaimed some months later, when James Henry had contrived to set up house with Emma in Liverpool, far from all acquaintances. Clearly my aunt and uncle viewed my father with disgust and repugnance, and this was not altogether uncongenial to me. The entire family, with the exception of her father, had erased Emma from their lives. However, much later Shad had begun to see his sister again, infrequently and in secret.

Through the years of unemployment and poverty James Henry had been obliged to pay the first Mrs Roe a continuing allowance. No wonder our financial difficulties had been so extreme. No wonder the strain had told on both my parents. No need to wonder now about that agonised 'Sake of Anne!'

'You remember that Bridlington holiday?' went on my uncle, surprisingly. 'That was when the first Mrs Roe died. It was a sort of honeymoon, you know.'

Was it? The dates, I discover, do not tally. The Bridlington holiday was eighteen months before their marriage. Perhaps there was some delay of which my uncle was unaware. Indeed, he had little to tell me beyond the bare facts. Of my father's first wife Shad knew nothing. Though they are assumed to have been childless, I still do not actually know that, and have no means of ascertaining. Nor have I ever discovered anything about the Roe family of Stoke, or what brought my father to Lancashire.

There are other puzzles. I have a certificate of baptism. The ceremony was conducted when I was three months old in an Anglican church in Hawarden in the county of Flint, an unlikely enough setting both geographically and denominationally. Both parents are named, though their signatures do not appear. Were they present? Did the Watsons arrange it? Even more intriguing: the officiating clergyman was one R. Gordon Roe. Had James Henry a relative in holy orders who could be persuaded to baptise his unacceptably illegitimate daughter? These are murky waters, into which I cannot peer.

## *ABOVE WATER*

Once upon a thousand lakes
our ancestors, not fools
at civil defence, drove stakes
down through yesterday pools;
unsteadily, maybe, built
their villages on stilts.

Anthropologists still
photograph them so –
this almost perverse will
to batten on what's below,
use, yet defy that element,
life's first environment.

Even through a seaside pier
you glimpse between plank and plank
that ancient, heaving, queer
summoning wetness, rank
with a sea salted smell,
that alien fall and swell.

The man from the oil rig told
of saunas, cinemas,
over implacable cold
forty-foot North Sea waves;
of a luxury dining room
somehow, bizarrely, home.

Told, too, how labourers feel
the mesmerising pull
of the huge central drill,

two miles of toughened steel
needling earth's mysteries
through water's enmities.

Into the mud of mind,
cesspit of memory
crawling with every kind
of dark micrology,
we thrust our piles, drive deep
drills into oily sleep.

Once upon a thousand dreams
our ancestors cast lines,
fishing for mirrored themes,
netting those myths that shrine
all we no longer know
of what may snarl below.

# 24. Reluctant guardians

It was around 5.00 a.m. when I wakened to the sound of raised voices. The landladies, dressing-gowned, were in the bathroom remonstrating with my father, who was shaving. When I appeared they sharply ordered me to deal with him, and retreated to their beds. My father was impatient. He had to catch his train, he insisted urgently.

'Train? Where to?'
'To Bury, of course. I've got to get to work.'

James Henry had slipped back more than twenty years, in the kind of time-loop so commonly experienced by the senile. It took me some time to persuade him to bed.

'He'll have to go,' declared the landladies the following day. 'He certainly can't stay here when you go back to work. We can't be expected to look after him. You must tell him he must leave.'

Their predicament was clear to me, and I sympathised. I did feel, though, that they should have the courage to tell their tenant to his face. This, they protested, they could not bear to do; it would be too cruel. In vain I told my father that he had notice to quit.

'Oh no.' he retorted firmly, and quite rationally. 'If they wanted me out they would say so. I know they wouldn't turn me out.' Vainly I remonstrated with both sides. Neither believed me. The days were ticking away, and I was still on unpaid leave from work.

Next came a summons from a friend of my mother's, to go and see her at once. I knew Dorothy slightly, an attractive divorcee in her forties, and went readily enough. She lived nearby.

172

Dorothy was in a rage. I was soundly berated for not keeping my father in check. It appeared that James Henry was pestering her with his attentions, using lewd and objectionable language. 'Lewd'? I could hardly credit it. That buttoned-up bowler-hatted ultra-respectable gent, J.H. Roe? Dorothy showed me letters, confused and foul, stuttered out with many mistypings on the faithful old portable Corona. So this was how he behaved when I was out. Later, as he lost control, I heard from his own lips more than enough to shock me.

Both Dorothy and the landladies were urging me to put my father into care. Trevor and I made enquiries. Somehow we found, not a rest home, but a cheap lodging house for the elderly – by a nice irony in the same street where I had been born. Almost by force we took him there, Trevor exerting all his kindly tact. James Henry was indignant, bewildered, but perforce submissive. We left him still protesting that his charming landladies would have him back soon.

Trevor's parents had friends with a removal and storage business. Quickly and cheaply the books and the sparse household effects were bundled into storage, and with relief I returned to Rochdale.

It was not long before James Henry's new landlord was as anxious to be rid of him as the genteel sisters had been, though with less excuse as he had specifically undertaken to care for a difficult old man. 'Get him out of here quickly,' I was bidden. How people do order one about, I thought, identifying with Alice in Wonderland. And indeed my world felt vaguely unreal, surreal, like a frustrating dream. A recommendation led us to accommodation only a few yards away. Once again it was the home of two sisters, but very unlike the earlier landladies. These were hard-spoken, hard-bargaining, hard-faced women, but I was at my wits' end and my father had literally been turned out. For money, they agreed to guard and nurse the hapless James Henry.

I was patient with my father, I think, but neither gentle nor kind.

Unreasonable anger still consumed me. All those plans I had had for my mother, after (as I had imagined it) my father's death! This man for whom I had twenty years' distaste, in spite of his undeniable affection for me; this man who had, in my view, wrecked my mother's life and hastened her death; was this man about to ruin my life also? Would I have to take him, at the very start of my married life, into my own household? Or must I defer marriage, continue to work, and devote my income to providing nursing care? A pathetic wreck of a human being he was; yet I could feel no pity, only aversion. At bottom I could not forgive him for being, after all, my father.

Further trouble soon developed. James Henry's new guardians found themselves unable to control his behaviour and unwilling to house him. Through a fraught month, they dispatched him to a geriatric hospital; sent me a bill for damage caused; confiscated his ancient typewriter, perhaps thinking it worth selling; and demanded reparation for a feather mattress destroyed by my father's incontinence.

Miss Hartley, throughout, had been a pillar of strength for me. Now she came into her own. When I handed her the letter about the mattress her indignation swelled.

'You are not to pay for it,' she declared. 'Those two harpies have had. enough out of you already. Leave this with me. I think I see a way out.'

When I returned from work the following evening Miss Hartley was gleeful. Her day's doings had filled her with wicked satisfaction. At that time, when the looms of Rochdale still clacked productively, there were, if you knew where to find them (and Miss Hartley did) little backstreet 'fent shops' where ends of fabric from the mills could be bought for pence. From one such, my scheming landlady had purchased a vast length of old fashioned striped cotton ticking. She had also – I no longer recall how – acquired an old, stained, but plump double-bed sized feather eiderdown.

'Very well: we'll replace their feather mattress all right. You'll see!'
Miss Hartley crowed happily.

The following day was spent by the avenging angel at her sewing
machine, creating out of the fent a single-sized mattress cover. On my
day off, the morning being fine, Miss Hartley took me out into her tiny
backyard. Now came the tricky stage of the operation, requiring four
hands. Carefully opening the feather quilt at one corner, we gently eased
the feathers a portion at a time – those that didn't fly off in the breeze –
into the new-made mattress cover, and hastily tacked down the opening.
Once firmly stitched, it was indubitably a single-sized feather mattress.
Next, Miss Hartley brought large sheets of brown paper, string and sticky
tape. With mischievous delight she organised the mailing of this strange
and bulky parcel to Blackpool.

'That'll settle them. They won't dare write to you again. Oh, but I'd
love to be there when they open it! I haven't enjoyed anything so much for
years.'

She was right. I heard no more from the complainants. What is more,
the mattress cover had not needed all the material, and from the remnants
Miss Hartley diligently sewed for my 'bottom drawer' (every prospective
bride in those days collected a 'bottom drawer') an apron, two tea-towels
and an ironing board cover: items which, she accurately estimated, were
worth more than the cost of the whole, so that the mattress, as it were,
cost nothing. Thrift was for my doughty mentor what self-control had
been for my mother: essential for effective living. Its exercise gave her
positive creative pleasure.

This incident shines in memory, a welcome frolic in a summer of anxiety.
In hospital my father declined rapidly, and died six months after my mother.
He died, I suppose, of a broken heart, the symptom of which was a broken
mind. The news came as, quite simply, a huge relief.

Shortly afterwards, Half-asleep Anne sat one afternoon in a storage warehouse, sorting through the pitiful collection of objects there and, by arrangement, dispatching anything useful to the YMCA across the road. Meticulously itemised by the removal men were those '3 painted wooden racks', James Henry's clumsily constructed but long cherished bookshelves. Their contents took longer to consider. A passing sigh for young Emma's still unread Everyman classics, their pages yellowed and the translations superseded. Having no room at Miss Hartley's for extra impedimenta, I selected only two books to keep, and with them a vase I liked and a plate with Shakespearean characters as a memento of Madame. Nothing stirred me until I reached her manuscript books, dog-eared hard-backed exercise books in which she had painstakingly transcribed the text of many of her recital passages. At that point only, hearing her voice in memory, I wept.

## 25. After-word

That was a period piece. Writing it was like performing a costume drama. One identifies with the characters but the clothes and manners are strange. So long ago, several lifetimes as it seems to me now, a girl who was I-and-not-I lived in those times, those places, with those people. Some speculate on a possible infinite series of alternative worlds, the nearest perhaps only a little different from ours. It is almost as though the girl who ran backwards inhabited one of those parallel worlds; while I, the woman who came to life at forty, happen to have her memory circuits.

I neither defend the girl nor judge her. She was foolish and hardhearted. She had fine aspirations and betrayed them. But neither do I write her story (in so far as it is her own story, for it is also that of her parents) as a confession. Guilt is much overrated. Anyway, it might turn the searchlight on an old woman's selfishness and folly – which, unlike the girl's, I should have to own. Rather, the writing of this memoir has been the act of a detached observer, murmuring with interest from time to time, 'Ah, so that is where I came from, is it?'

Nor am I shaking any admonitory finger at the young, and certainly not seeking to warn them. It is pointless to warn the young about life; they must thread their way through their own, different, mazes. If I have a word for the young, it is one of hope and confidence. You need never be altogether lost to yourself! It is possible in later life to gather the scattered fragments, the chaotic debris, the sheer dullness, and out of these unlikely materials to create an integrated self, both purposeful and reposeful. Yes, I believe in resurrection: not in any magic after-death resuscitation, but in fresh starts, fresh momentum in this life.

That faith arises from my own experience. A reader may well ask how it squares with the apparently sad stories of Emma and James Henry. In fact, it does. Their perspective would be different from mine; they would have told their story differently. Emma, driven to ground by what at that time and in her milieu was a disgraceful pregnancy, in fact re-emerged triumphantly in later years as the much-admired Madame. I know she found delight and fulfilment in her career, as well as cherishing her daughter and her own state of motherhood. I cannot even guess at James Henry's early life; there were hints of a troubled family background, and one supposes his first marriage was unsuccessful. Yet in mid-life his love for Emma blossomed, and never lost its intensity. In spite of all the hardships, his joy in their partnership was apparent even to me.

In our disordered world there are too many tragic lives in which this kind of redemption has no chance. That is shamefully true, and the most cogent reason for resisting war, violence and capital punishment. Yet we may ponder T.S. Eliot's percipient lines in *The Dry Salvages (Four Quartets)*:
> The torment of others remains an experience
> Unqualified, unworn by subsequent attrition.
'The torment of *others* . . .' What do we know of the inner experience of others? Each knows in what ways her own distress has been mitigated. All but the most terrible of lives have lit moments, forms of relief, times when suffering is ameliorated by simple delights. For all, inherent in being human there is the possibility of redemption.

Hans Andersen's Tin Soldier fell (if I recall the story correctly) into the gutter on a rainy day. He was put to sail in a paper boat, which plunged into a drain. Lost to sight, carried into far waters, swallowed by a fish, the soldier at last emerged when a cook cut open the fish in her kitchen. Resurrected, he found himself at home: the same tin soldier yet not the same. The tale is a children's version of the Odyssey, the myth of anyone's life journey. After the Trojan War Odysseus struggles towards home. Ithaca is not all that far away, yet through perils and adventures the seafaring wanderer is tossed from place to place for ten years. One day, exhausted, shipwrecked on an unknown shore, he awakes, collects

himself, and recognises Ithaca. There are problems ahead, but he is home
and again Odysseus.

# NOT AS THE CROW FLIES

I am no crow but an old bewildered man
heavy with meaning and meaning.
Crows fly straight they say, but a thousand miles
was a ten year stretch. Preening
its glossy achievement a crow might have missed much.
From Troy to Ithaca there's sea, there's land.
I sprawl on sand
grateful not to be skyborn: knowing my place.

Knowing this place: sand on an idle palm
spilling a welcome, gritting
a real floor. Surf with a sawfish edge
scallops a greeting.
Once upon a Lotos time – O Ithaca,
how they erased you! Cry the name aloud,
Ithaca! – you were cloud,
cloud of unknowing, dimmer than memory.

Memory's dim . . . an old bewildered man.
Who's in the cave there, loathing
that one-eyed ignorance? Odysseus or Oudeis,
Nobody? Nothing?
We were sheep . . . we have followed too much . . . and we escaped
without identity. Parade in line.

Who are these swine
snuffling in Circe's filth? Where's Nobody?

Less than Nobody, no body may become.
Let slip identity, abandon vision,
still there's a lodestone, somewhere Ithaca.
Held in a rope prison
we'll hear the Sirens out. They'll sing your soul
into a foreign frenzy, wind the sound
stranglescarf round
your drowning neck; but better to have heard,

to have heard the clashing rocks, to have smelt the salt
dry on the skin's ageing,
lingered with languorous Calypso, rowed against
the Aegean's raging.
This was my coming, goddess, this your urging.
Scrub from my eyes these Trojan cataracts!
This shore . . . these tracks . . .
sweet Ithaca! my homing, my enlarging.

'My enlarging.' In a sense now obsolete, *enlarging* meant being set free from prison. In the current sense, it indicates widening horizons. I mean it both ways, for that was my experience.

A wide-awake nine-year-old set her inner alarm clock for forty. Half-asleep Anne dozed from twenty-three to approaching forty. Then something stirred. What, said Anne to Anne, yawning and stretching, became of Anne?

When the ageing body awakes in bed (I am now sixty-five and beginning to know something of this) there are discomforts. Pressure points protest. Shoulder, ear, hip or leg has taken the weight. There may be aches, shooting pains, cramps. This may serve as metaphor. Mentally, emotionally, it was like that at forty. There were painful processes in the rediscovery of myself. Or let us say it was rebirth, and birth is a messy business. It was renaissance, and the Renaissance was a disturbing time as well as exhilarating. Gradually, soul capacities long atrophied creaked into activity. It became possible to feel, to wonder, to love, to write, to renew the religious quest. I made blunders, I fumbled and stumbled, had much belatedly to learn; but I was alive. A monochrome world blazed into colour. Bushes began to burn.

That awakening was a quarter of a century ago. I am more fortunate than my mother, having already been given longer. The defensive old cliché, 'Life begins at forty', was actually true for me. Of these latter years, the best and most interesting of my life, I do not write here. They are not part of this tale. Besides, they are peopled with friends still alive, of whom I could not write because I am too close to them: happily. The best wine, like miraculous transformed water, has been kept until the last.

# CANA

The first hearthstone stays the true stone,
    they say.
Roots tug the cut flower,
    they say.
View from a child's window landscapes lifelong
an inner eye, they say –

    but –

A found hearthstone is the truest stone,
        some say.
Cuttings strike the freshest roots,
        some say.
Land loved latest is a dug-for garden,
  some with spades say –

        so –

Some prospectors strike their El Dorado,
        I say.
Storm rainbows end in treasure trove,
        I say.
The finest wine was poured from water jars
late in the feast, I say.

# BIOGRAPHICAL NOTE

Anne Ashworth is retired and lives in Blackpool where most of her life has been spent. She was for twenty-one years librarian of a sixth-form college, and concurrently for ten years reviews editor of *Reform*. Now an active Quaker, she edits the Quaker *Universalist*. About a hundred of her poems have appeared in poetry magazines and anthologies. Though a 'slim volume' entitled *Mirrorwork* was published by Envoi Poets most of her poetry remains uncollected. She is a member of far too many high-principled associations intent on improving the world, but also finds time for the delights of friendship and the frustrations of amateur painting.